THE COMPLETE GUIDE TO THE BICHON FRISE

Rachel Kass and Kris Wolfe

Publication Data

Rachel Kass and Kris Wolfe

The Complete Guide to the Bichon Frise ---- First edition.

Summary: "Successfully raising a Bichon Frise dog from puppy to old age" --- Provided by publisher.

ISBN: 978-1-952069-10-9

[1. Bichon Frise Dogs --- Non-Fiction] I. Title.

This book has been written with the published intent to provide accurate and authoritative information in regard to the subject matter included. While every reasonable precaution has been taken in preparation of this book the author and publisher expressly disclaim responsibility for any errors, omissions, or adverse effects arising from the use or application of the information contained inside. The techniques and suggestions are to be used at the reader's discretion and are not to be considered a substitute for professional veterinary care. If you suspect a medical problem with your dog, consult your veterinarian.

Design by Sorin Rădulescu

First paperback edition, 2020

Kris Wolfe bio photo courtesy of: L Photography/Lindsey Wimmer-Cohen

TABLE OF CONTENTS

CHAPTER 1
The History of the Bichon Frise and General Breed Information

The Bichon Frise is a fun, family-friendly dog breed which has ties as far back as the 14th century and has quite the adventurous breed history. Unlike some dog breeds that have always been and will always be used for the same thing, such as hunting or herding, Bichons have jumped around from fishing dogs to the preferred dog of European nobles and even dabbled in being circus show dogs for a while.

Why would this specific breed have such a varied history? Bichons have a range of unique qualities, but the one that sets them apart is their jovial and animated personality. They love to goof around, be cute, and be the center of attention. It also means they adapt well to different situations and are willing to go anywhere as long as they are loved.

The ancestors of the Bichon were called Barbets and were from the Mediterranean. Poodles, Maltese, and Caniche are also all descendants of the Barbet species, though the breeds likely split off sometime in the 1300s. The original name of the Bichon was actuallyBarbichon, which was then shortened. There were actually four different breeds of Barbichon: Bichon Bolognese, Bichon Havanese, Bichon Tenerife, and Bichon Maltese.

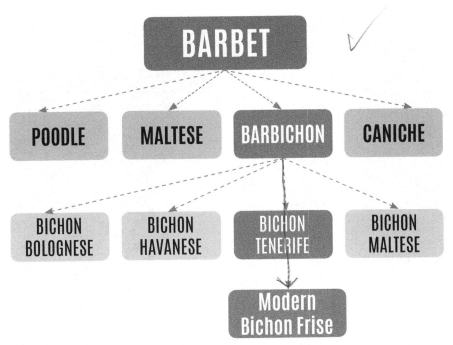

In the 1300s, Bichon Tenerifes were very popular with Italian nobility, who would give the dogs a lion-style cut. As the breed's popularity increased, Italian merchants and other middle-class workers also started to appreciate the Bichon's fun and playful nature.

After France invaded Italy in the late 1400s, Italian influence started moving north. And, after witnessing the huge personalities of the Italians' small adorable dogs, the French wanted a piece of the pie. Soon, Bichons could be spotted across the laps of both French and Italian nobles and were even the favorite pet of several kings, including King Francis I and King Henry III in the 1500s. It has been said that King Henry III loved his dog so much he carried the Bichon in a basket that hung from his neck.

As time went on, the Bichon's popularity grew, and not just with nobles. By the 19th century, the Bichon was considered a common dog and was loved by

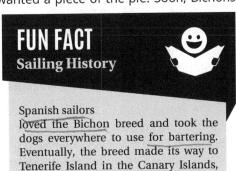

FUN FACT
Sailing History

Spanish sailors loved the Bichon breed and took the dogs everywhere to use for bartering. Eventually, the breed made its way to Tenerife Island in the Canary Islands, where the breed was further refined until it was discovered by Italian sailors in the 1300s and brought back to Italy. There, the dogs became beloved companions of royalty around Europe.

Photo Courtesy of
Michael Tortorete

everyone from nobles to street performers. As a result, Bichons actually had quite a bit of success as street performers and circus dogs in the 1800s. Their fun disposition and lovable nature made them entertaining to all.

The World Wars were tough on Bichons, as the countries where they were most prominent were at the heart of those wars. Many Bichons found themselves on the streets. A handful of Bichon lovers rescued many of the homeless dogs and quite possibly saved the breed.

Bichons did not come to the United States until 1955. The Bichon became part of the American Kennel Club in 1972 and started showing in the non-sporting group in 1973. A Bichon won the breed's first and only Best in Show at the Westminster Kennel Club Dog Show in 2001.

Physical Characteristics

Bichons are always white and tend to weigh between 12 and 18 pounds. Bichons also always have black eyes and a black button nose. They don't usually stand more than a foot tall, though there are some that are slightly larger who might break the 12-inch mark. A unique aspect of the Bichon is that they have hair, not fur. This means their hair needs to be cut and brushed like a human's; however, they do not shed as much as most dogs, making them great pets for those with allergies. A Bichon's hair is curly and when brushed has a "powder puff" appearance. Their tails curve over their backs and most owners keep the tail hair long, which increases the cute and poofy look.

What Does It Mean to Be Hypoallergenic?

Bichon Frises tend to be considered hypoallergenic dogs, as they shed very little and have hair instead of fur. Nevertheless, if you or a family member has allergies to animals, be sure to spend some time around Bichons prior to adopting or purchasing one. It is also advisable to consult your allergist or doctor before acquiring a dog.

Photo Courtesy of Cindy Cho

Behavioral Characteristics

"Bichons are very animated and have huge personalities. Most are happy-go-lucky, confident, and thrive on praise."

Vicki Turner
Turner Dog Ranch

Photo Courtesy of Diana Capone

Though quite small, Bichons are known for having some of the biggest personalities in the dog world. Obviously, their lovability caught the attention of nobles throughout history and it is no surprise why. Bichons have a bubbly personality, love to please, and enjoy being the center of attention. One breeder describes them as "smart little dogs." Bichons are just happy dogs with a great disposition. They tend to be described as merry, cheerful, sociable, sensitive, affectionate, and intelligent. Additionally, Bichons love to play with kids and do tricks and tend to get along with other pets or animals.

Because Bichons love to please, they generally are very trainable. They do not do well with negative reinforcement or yelling though. Due to their playful personality, it is important to continue training them throughout their lives as it is something they love to do. While each dog is different, as a breed, Bichons are easy to train with constant, positive reinforcement. They want to be your best friend and please you, so training can be a great bonding experience between you and your dog.

Is a Bichon Frise the Right Fit for You?

Throughout the book we will continue to expand on Bichons, the characteristics of the breed, and how they might fit in your family; however, it is good to do an early litmus test to see if a Bichon might be the right fit for your family. There are a few keys to the Bichon. First, they love to be around people and tend to have separation anxiety. If you travel a lot or plan to leave your dog alone for long periods of time, a Bichon might not be the right fit. They are not the type of dog that can entertain themselves or be happy lounging alone all day; they want to be by your side. Second, Bichons can be high energy. While they don't need to run for miles every day, they do love to play and will need to be exercised daily. Third, Bichons need to be groomed about every two months, usually by a professional groomer. Their hair can get matted and therefore they need to be brushed regularly. They do require a bit more maintenance than the general dog. Bichons truly are amazing family dogs. They will likely be the best companion you have ever had and they love children and other pets, but it is important to make sure that they fit well in your lifestyle.

FUN FACT
Royal Companions

Royalty around Europe loved Bichons. King Henry III of France loved his Bichons so much that he carried them in a ribbon-covered basket tied around his neck.

CHAPTER 2
Choosing a Bichon Frise

Buying vs. Adopting

When choosing to get a dog, sometimes the biggest decision can be whether to buy or adopt your new family member. This can be a tough choice as there are benefits and downsides to both. Here we will discuss some of the differences between buying and adopting.

Buying

Buying a dog or puppy can be quite a financial investment, though the cost can vary based on the breeder. Additionally, reputable breeders do not have puppies available all the time and tend to have waiting lists to get a dog. Both of these can be inconveniences. That said, buying a dog from a breeder does have its benefits. First, you will likely know the bloodline of the dog, and if you ever want to show your dog, having a documented history and a good bloodline is key. Second, when buying from a breeder you will probably be able to interact with the parents of the puppy to get an idea of the personality the puppy might grow up to have. Buying a dog definitely allows for you to have a lot more information, but could be expensive and might require patience and possibly travel to get the dog.

Photo Courtesy of Katie Linacre

Adopting

Adopting a dog that needs a home is a great option, especially if you do not plan to show the dog and just want a great companion or family pet. Adopting dogs tends not to be as expensive as purchasing a dog or puppy, but you have less control over a dog's age or gender. For instance, it can be hard to find a Bichon Frise puppy to adopt as there are not many out there, but there are adult dogs who need a loving home. If you have a young family, then getting an adult dog is probably a good option. The main downside to adopting is that you do not know the history of the dog. Don't let the idea of not knowing the dog's history scare you, as most rescues do in-home fostering so you will know the dog's temperament and usually if they are good with kids and other pets.

There are other benefits of adopting as well. If you are considering adopting a Bichon, ask to foster first. This will give you the opportunity to get to know the dog and allow it to interact with your other pets. Additionally, the shelters and rescue agency typically do a health check with a veterinarian, give needed shots, provide a rabies certificate, and may also spay or neuter the dog before adoption. In some cases, they will arrange the spay/neuter surgery in advance and ask if you are willing to take them to their appointment and care for them during recovery.

My personal experience with adopting a Bichon was excellent. He was a wonderful fit to our family and was even accepted by our older Boxer, who in her senior years has become less accepting of strange dogs. Also, since Ricky was nearly a year old when we adopted him, he was mostly potty trained. After an adjustment period and some positive reinforcement, he became fully trained and an irreplaceable part of our family.

How to Find a Reputable Breeder

It is extremely important to find a reputable breeder for several reasons. A reputable breeder will not overbreed their dogs in hopes of making more money and will treat all of their dogs well. The puppies will spend their time with their mom and not locked in a cage. Additionally, reputable breeders will make sure the puppies are healthy, well taken care of, and old

Photo Courtesy of
Sally Wegher

enough to wean from their mothers before separating them. This is as opposed to how dogs are treated at puppy mills.

Most dogs in pet stores are from puppy mills—mass breeding animal farms. A lot of dogs that come from puppy mills have serious illnesses, both short and long term. They are raised in awful conditions and overbred. The puppies are separated from their mothers far too early, which can cause both behavioral and health problems. Because of the poor conditions, puppy mills won't allow potential buyers to see the puppies at the farms. Due to the negative stigma attached to puppy mills, they have gotten creative with marketing by selling puppies online, directly to the customer, sight unseen, often via shipment of the pet. The puppy mills have also become crafty at appearing to be a boutique, or small, family-owned operation, by creating multiple websites that each appear to be quaint and wholesome operations, versus the mass breeding of multiple breeds of dogs simultaneously with little concern for the comfort and health of the animals.

While finding a reputable breeder can be tricky, it is an important step. The best place to start researching breeders is online on reputable sites only. The American Kennel Club has a list of reputable breeders with links to their specific websites and contact information. Additionally, the Bichon Frise Club of America has some great breeder resources as well.

After an initial online search, it is time to take the research offline. The next step is calling the breeders, asking questions, and setting up an appointment to see their home. This is a critical step. Without seeing the puppy in the home it is being raised or seeing the home before the puppy is being born, it is impossible to tell if the breeder is actually reputable.

When you visit, it is important to ask questions such as requesting references from families who have purchased puppies, veterinary records for your puppy, and permission to see all of the spaces where the dogs spend their time. Breeders should encourage you to spend time with the mom of the puppies as well as visit the puppies themselves several times. A good breeder wants a good home for their puppies so they will likely do an interview of sorts with you as well.

Research, talking on the phone, and visiting a facility are the three biggest steps to finding a reputable breeder. It might take time to find the right fit, but it will be worth the effort in the end.

Health Tests and Certifications

A reputable breeder will provide you with quite a bit of paperwork with your puppy. First, you should get all of their vet records including visits and vaccinations. Second, you should receive a written health guarantee from the breeder that you should thoroughly read through. Third, you should receive a birth certificate that includes the parents of your puppy. The breeder should have on hand information regarding the potential for genetic problems such as hip dysplasia, knee problems, or diseases of the vital organs. The best way to get the information is to have the parents and grandparents of the puppy tested, which most reputable breeders will already have done and will be able to provide documentations for.

Breeder Contracts and Guarantees

Good breeders want to make sure their dogs go to good homes. The same is true for you as an owner; you want to make sure your dog comes from a high-quality breeder to limit the possibility for health or behavioral problems.

The breeder will likely ask you questions such as why you want a dog, who your vet will be, and a list of all of the people in your household. You will also be asked to sign a contract stating that you will spay or neuter the puppy when they are old enough unless you are using the dog for show. Another contract you will sign is that if you cannot keep the dog, you will return it to the breeder.

You should receive a health guarantee. The health guarantee will differ from breeder to breeder so it is important that you read and understand the "guarantee" completely, not only in terms of what conditions the guarantee covers, but for how long and under what circumstances the coverage is valid. Additionally, the guarantee may only cover the replacement of the puppy, not medical bills, shipping, or fees related to the death of the pet. Remember that if both parties are signing the guarantee, you have also entered into a contract with the seller and are therefore agreeing to their terms as well, which may leave with you fewer options than what you may desire. Therefore, if you have concerns about the breeder or the health of the puppy, do not rely on the guarantee to cover all possible outcomes. Instead, keep searching for a breeder and a puppy that you are confident in. Be careful not to give in to high-pressure tactics when choosing a breeder.

Choosing Your Perfect Pup

"Breeders can usually match up the temperament and personality of the puppy to match the needs of the family who is interested in finding a puppy."

Betsy Savage
Dazzling Bichons

The most important part of choosing your pup is to have a personal connection with him or her. Spend time with the puppy and really try to notice the differences between different puppies. Even at such a young age when their personalities are still developing, you can get glimpses of the adult dog they will become through spending time with them. Also, ask questions about the puppies' demeanors throughout their short lives. The breeder will have been with the litter from the start and know little things about each of the dogs. It is important to go in with an open mind; sometimes dogs surprise you and you might get attached to a male when you thought you wanted a female. Have fun when you are choosing, and relax. If you are relaxed, the dogs probably will be too.

Other factors to consider are personality traits that you prefer and that match your lifestyle. If you are an avid traveler or if you like to take your dog everywhere with you, you might consider the puppy that readily hopped in your lap, versus the one who was hiding during your visit. If you are a homebody, a shy dog may suit you just fine. While their personality is going to develop and change over time, a lot can be deduced from spending time with each puppy during the visit.

HELPFUL TIP
Color Matters

Bichons are always completely white with a black nose and eyes. Apricot, buff, or cream are allowed around the ears. If anybody is trying to sell you a dog as a Bichon that isn't all white, run away. The dog is either a mutt or poorly bred.

Tips for Adopting or Buying a Bichon Frise

Hopefully, you have learned a lot in this chapter about adopting your new family member. Here are some final tips for adopting your puppy.

1. Make sure your house is prepared before you bring the puppy home. That way, when you get home you can just bond with your puppy instead of scrambling to get everything ready. This is discussed in detail in the following chapter.

2. Be prepared for some bumps in the road. Puppies are adorable, but they also need a lot of care. Be prepared to get up in the middle of the night or for some accidents around the house. This is all part of them growing up.

3. Be patient. Good breeders and even some rescues don't always have puppies or dogs available. Sometimes there is even a wait list; however, finding your perfect pup is worth the wait.

4. Make it a family affair. If you have kids or a significant other, make sure everyone in the family meets the dog before you adopt or buy it.

CHAPTER 3
Preparing Your Home for Your Bichon Frise

Adjusting Your Current Pets and Children

Bringing a new family member home can be a challenge, especially if you have children or other pets. It is important to introduce them correctly and in a safe environment. Improper introduction of the new pet could lead to it being scared or not adjusting well. If you have kids it is extremely important to teach them how to be safe and respectful with a dog's personal space. While Bichons are extremely well mannered, moving to a new home is stressful and they might get agitated.

It is important to teach your kids to let the dog sniff their hand before petting the dog. This ensures the dog has some control and also shows respect for their space. Also, it is key to have them approach from the front and not surprise the dog from behind. Similar to humans, dogs don't like being startled. While it is very unlikely that a Bi-

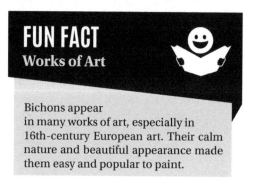

FUN FACT
Works of Art

Bichons appear in many works of art, especially in 16th-century European art. Their calm nature and beautiful appearance made them easy and popular to paint.

chon will growl or snap if startled from behind, it could increase their stress level or get them overexcited. These simple actions are even more imperative to teach your kids if you are adopting an adult dog. Puppies tend to be more go with the flow, but an adult dog might be a bit stressed.

Introducing pets should also be handled with care. With other pets, specifically cats or other dogs in the house, you need to be aware of the stress levels of both the new dog and the existing pets. It is critical that you are fully engaged the entire time and that you notice if one or both of the pets get stressed or intimidated. If this happens, it is important to separate them and try again later.

If you are introducing your current dog to a new adult dog (versus a puppy) try to enlist the help of a significant other or friend. It works best if dogs meet in neutral territory, so taking the dogs for a walk and having them meet tends to work well. It can also be beneficial to tire each of the dogs out before having them meet. This way they don't have a ton of pent-up energy. If one of the dogs doesn't tend to do well meeting dogs when on a leash, then try to have them meet off leash in a neutral area like a park or friend's yard. If you are introducing a puppy to your resident dog, your puppy may be cautious or fearful. Conversely, it may be ready to romp and play. It's important that you understand the personality of your original dog to determine how they may react to one another. Regardless of personalities, however, your close supervision is required until you are certain that they are both fully comfortable.

Once the dogs have met, then you can take them back to your house, but keep them separated. If your resident dog has a favorite room or place to hang out, then put them there so they are relaxed the entire time. If either of the dogs is crate trained then you could put them in their crate as well. Depending on how the dogs are doing, you could do a few more structured walks or planned interactions before letting them meet in the house. If you are bringing home a young puppy, these additional steps may not be required.

When they meet in the house make sure you are around. Let them sniff each other and give them a little bit of space. Just be sure to be ready in case one of the dogs gets scared. Even if they are getting along, I would not leave them alone unsupervised for a while. If you leave for work and they are crate trained, then you could keep them in their crates.

A great way to help with possible stress levels is to use pheromones. This is a chemical which can be sprayed and which can naturally calm animals. There are different pheromones that work for dogs and cats, and they are available at most pet stores and online. These products are used to decrease stress and general anxiety and can be used in a plug-in device in your home or you can purchase a pheromone collar for your pet. Look for products with a long history of verified reviews that are mostly positive. Discuss the products with your vet, or ask your vet for a specific recommendation. You may also ask the manager of a trusted boarding facility, if you have one that you use, as many facilities use pheromones in their facility. It is important to note, though, that pheromones are not to be used to treat aggression and are only part of an overall plan for reducing stress and anxiety in your pets. Additionally, they may or may not work for your pet, so try the products out in advance.

Dangerous Things Your Dog Might Eat

HELPFUL TIP
Are Bichons Hypoallergenic?

While no dog breed is truly hypoallergenic—people are allergic to the dander and saliva of a dog, rather than its fur—many people with allergies are okay around Bichons since they don't shed. People with allergies should spend some time with a Bichon before getting one to be sure that their allergies aren't triggered.

If you already have a dog or have had a dog in the past, you know they will eat pretty much anything they see, especially if you have a puppy. Puppies, not unlike babies, love to explore by chewing and tasting as many things as possible. It is important to be aware of anything dangerous that is within reach of your dog or puppy. Most dangerous things your dog might eat will be some form of human food, plant, or cleaning supply. Let's review hazardous items or products room by room, keeping in mind that a determined Bichon can often be very creative when he or she wants to get into something:

Kitchen

- Cleaning supplies and dishwasher pods (lock the cabinet with a child lock)
- Food items in plastic bags like bread or buns; if ingested, the bag could become twisted in their intestines
- Snack foods that might sit out in a bowl that may contain chocolate, tree nuts, or artificial sweeteners
- Food or drink items in lower cabinets should be moved higher
- Coffee packs, K-cups, or other caffeinated beverage items
- The trash should be blocked off or away from your dog's reach; we call our Bichon a trash panda because if there is access, he is going in
- Meat bones after meals

Bathrooms

- Cleaning supplies
- Personal hygiene products including toothpaste
- Bobby pins, safety pins, and other small items that fall on the floor and are easily missed when cleaning
- Bath salts
- Medications, including gummy or chewy vitamins (put in a locking container or a cabinet up high); check for dropped pills as well

Photo Courtesy of
Lisa Palermo

- Makeup and skincare products

Laundry room or cleaning closet

- Detergent pods
- Dryer sheets (new or used)
- Mop water (never leave cleaning water out for dogs to drink or potentially fall into)
- Clothes pins
- Cleaning supplies
- Dry-cleaning bags (suffocation risk)
- Plastic or wooden hangers on the floor (they will likely chew these into small pieces)
- Sewing supplies

Bedroom or dressing closet

- Jewelry
- Purses or gym bags containing gum, deodorant, snack bars, etc.
- Shoes or inserts
- Moth balls
- Stuff you have put under your bed and forgotten about, or things that have fallen under the bed

Common living spaces

- Plants, especially toxic ones like aloe, calla lilies, alocasia, dieffenbachia, adenium, geranium, English ivy, peace lily, oleander, brunfelsia, and cacti
- Keys and wallets
- Candy bowls
- CDs and DVDs
- Coins
- Dog food, dog treats, and dog supplements
- Toys or puzzles, especially with small pieces and parts
- Batteries (loose, in the pack, or in items like remotes)
- Ink pens and pencils
- Bug sprays and pesticides

Other Household Dangers

It is impossible to get rid of all of the dangers in your house, but doing your best to prevent them will help keep your dog healthy, and the vet bills low. The first thing to check is if there is anything sharp that is in your dog's range. If you have a basement or workshop area that the dog may have access to, then make sure it is clean and organized so that your pup doesn't step on anything sharp like a nail. If keeping your workshop or garage space clean is just not realistic, keep it double barricaded, meaning that you should keep the door closed but also block off access to the door with a baby gate placed in a hall-way or nearby access point in case

Photo Courtesy of Melissa Platt.

someone doesn't close the door completely. In addition to obvious hazards like antifreeze, there are hundreds of common items found in garages that could be extremely dangerous or lethal to your pets, especially if ingested.

Preparing a Space for Your Dog Inside

Similar to humans, a lot of dogs like to have a home base. Crate training is very popular and gives a dog their own space or bedroom of sorts. The key is to get a crate just big enough for your puppy, but also able to expand for your adult dog. Some people crate train their dogs when they are puppies and then when they are older leave the dog out of the crate full time, but give it the option to go into the crate if it wants. If you plan to use a crate to potty train your Bichon, purchase a crate that is only large enough for your dog to stand, turn around, sleep, eat and drink water in it. The reason for this is because Bichons want to be clean, so by creating a small space, you are encouraging them not to soil their personal living quarters. You can also purchase a crate with an adjustable divider so the crate can "grow" with your puppy. If you already have a crate, and it doesn't have a divider, but is too big to keep your Bichon confined to a small enough space, consider adding a box or container to the inside of the crate to take up space. Just make sure that it is not something that your pet can chew up or ingest. We will discuss more on crate training in Chapter 5.

In addition to choosing a crate (if you will be using a crate at all), consider the following important lifestyle questions:

- Where will my puppy or dog be while I am at work or away?
- In what room will it sleep? Do I want it in the bed with me? What does my partner think?
- If the dog barks, who will it disturb? Who will be getting up at night with the puppy if needed?
- Is the space I want to keep the dog well ventilated and safe?
- Will I allow my new dog on the furniture?
- Will I be using store-bought food or making food?
- What is the puppy or dog currently eating where they are? Will the current owners or shelter be giving me any of this food, or do I need to buy some to use or mix in with their new food I plan to feed them?
- Where and how will I store my dog's food? Where will he or she eat and drink?
- Does the dog have any special needs, phobias, or fears?
- Can the new dog navigate the stairs safely or will I need to block them off for now?
- Will the areas that my other pets prefer become common and shared spaces between the old and new pets, or do I need to separate them in some way?
- Can my furniture handle some possible chewing or accidents, or do I need to cover it with blankets or upholstery spray? Or do I need to store some treasured or irreplaceable pieces that I can't stand to have ruined?
- Who else, like my kids or spouse, do I need to talk to about keeping their spaces tidy and safe, or at least keeping their doors closed at all times?
- What is my policy on feeding my puppy or dog scraps or human food? Who else needs to be a part of this conversation?

Careful preparation, planning, and communication within your home can help make bringing your new puppy or dog home a healthy and low-stress experience. Because Bichons are so bright and determined, even crafty, it is unlikely that you can go overboard preparing your living space, and your roommate or family, for their arrival.

Preparing Outside Spaces

Outside spaces can be a bit trickier than indoor spaces because there are many factors that may feel outside of your control, simply because you might not be aware of some hidden hazards on your property. But just like when preparing the inside of your home for your new Bichon, there is a method to the process that will make it easier to prepare your outdoor space for safe living. We will go area by area to help you prepare your outdoor space properly for your arriving Bichon puppy or dog:

Porches, decks, and balconies

- Check for loose boards, mortar, or splinters.
- Check under porches or decks for dangerous items that have fallen underneath.
- Check for loose railings and spindles.
- Remove any items that have been sitting outside but do not need to be there.
- Remove high-value items that you don't want chewed like wicker furniture, seat cushions, and pillows, until you feel that you can trust your dog not to chew them up.

Landscaping, natural vegetation and water features

- Check your landscaping for poisonous plants or poison ivy, oak, or sumac. You may have to have these plants professionally removed.
- Check for sharp, ragged, or splintered roots that could impale their paw or that they might trip over while walking or playing.
- Repair holes in the dirt that they could fall into while running and playing.
- Dispose of old hay or straw that could be moldy and toxic.
- Store or remove holiday decorations, broken planters, or trash.
- Empty containers that have filled with rainwater that may be contaminated or that may attract mosquitoes to your property.
- Refrain from using lawn chemicals that could irritate their skin or paws.
- Block access to water features.

Fences and gates

- With a pair of boots on, walk around and kick each plank of wooden fencing. Tighten loose boards.

- Walk around chain-link fencing, kicking the bottom of the fence for weak spots. Add a tension wire or a bottom rail to the fencing if needed. Fill holes under the fence's edge with rocks and dirt and pat down firmly. Use pavers under areas where dogs are more likely to dig. Use zip ties for a quick repair to detached areas.

- Add carabiner clips to gate clips, or add combination locks to the gates if you are concerned about theft of your dog.

- In some areas, coyotes are a viable threat. If so, you might look into installing coyote spinners to the tops of your fences. These spinning, horizontal bars are positioned along the top rail of your fence, making it difficult for animals to enter or exit your yard easily.

Sheds, barns, chicken coops, and crawlspaces

- Carefully check inside and outside sheds and barns for hazards.

- If you store chemicals, fuel, or poison, or if there is rodent poison present, you should keep these buildings locked at all times.

- Use a combination lock on crawlspace access doors.

- Secure all entry points that are not fully secure.

Driveway and parking areas

- Remove trash and secure trashcans.

- Pick up screws, bolts, or other small choking hazards.

- Clean up oil spots or areas of spilled chemicals.

- Secure chicken coops or hen houses.

Recreation and social spaces

- Check bonfire or fire pits for dangerous or sharp items, including smashed aluminum cans.

- Make sure propane tanks are closed at the valve.

- Put away the grill utensils.

- Block access to saunas, hot tubs, and pools.

Pest control

- Always check with your pest control company before using flea, tick, or mosquito treatments on your lawn to make sure that they are pet safe, including for the age of your pet.

- If you have the outside of the home sprayed for spiders or other pests, ask about the safety of these chemicals for your puppy or dog.

Photo Courtesy of
Pat Rossi

You will also need to determine how you will secure your dog when it is outside. You will need to determine the type of physical fence you would like, or have an underground and invisible fence installed. You can also use a radio fence that operates off a radio signal from a device inside your home. You will also need to consider shade, shelter, water access, and threats from harm from people, other dogs, coyotes, or even hawks. Additionally, you need to be aware of the safety and shelter laws for your city and/or county, as well as your local leash laws. It is never advisable to let your Bichons roam unsupervised, due to the risk of injury, theft, or even death. Additionally, mindfully weigh the risks of using a "tie-out" in your yard, as there are many risks to your dog if he or she is tied in place and unable to run from predators.

CHAPTER 4
Bringing Home Your Bichon Frise

The Importance of Having a Plan

Bringing a puppy or dog home for the first time could be chaotic or stressful, so having a plan can help limit some of the stress on both you and the dog. Here are some things that should be included in your plan:

- What to buy and why
- How you will introduce other pets or kids
- Introducing your new Bichon to its new space
- Knowing what general rules you will have for your dog (rooms they can or cannot go in, if they can jump on furniture, etc.)
- Who will be responsible for feeding and caring for the pet? Will this be in shifts or alternating turns?
- How quickly do we need to see the vet for a checkup?

Photo Courtesy of
Tammy Capozzoli

Photo Courtesy of Nancy Byrne

Pet Supplies to Have Ready

Shopping for your new Bichon can be exciting and fun! There are so many great products to choose from. If you want to bargain shop, check online for some gently used options. Also, many shelters have a store that contains used or new donated items for a lower cost. Also, remember that your new Bichon is more interested in cuddles and kisses than how much money you spend on them. At the end of this section I will list your "must have" items and some bargain options to help you settle in with your new pup without breaking the bank.

- **Leash** – Start with a basic, lightweight leash around 6 feet in length. Until you and your dog have bonded, and they have learned basic obedience, they do not need a long or retractable leash, which will lack the structure that an untrained dog needs in the beginning.

- **Harness** – Choose a harness that fits now, not one that they can grow into, as you don't want to take any chances that your dog could slip out of it. A harness is best for training your dog on a leash, as it is more difficult for your small Bichon to slip out of.

- **Collar** – Even if you have a harness, you will need to choose a well-fitting collar for your Bichon. And extra small is a good bet for a puppy. This is not the time to invest in an expensive or fashion collar. Be practical. Your puppy will likely grow, and an adult Bichon may gain or lose weight after moving in with you. You will need to securely attach the dog's name tag and rabies tag to this collar. Make sure it fits properly and that no more than two fingers can slide under the collar when your Bichon is wearing it. The collar should fit like a necktie, not like a necklace.

HELPFUL TIP
Pet Insurance

Bichons can live for quite a long time, even reaching their late teen years, but that's a lot of time for accidents and illnesses to occur. Can you afford emergency vet care for your Bichon? Pet insurance can help you recoup some of the money you pay for emergency vet care, but there are waiting periods for it to take effect after you sign up, and plans always exclude preexisting conditions, so the time to sign up for pet insurance is as soon as you bring your Bichon home.

- **Bowls** – Stainless steel bowls are affordable and last forever. Plastic bowls can get chewed up. Glass or crockery bowls are more likely to be broken. Two eight-ounce bowls will likely meet the needs of a young or adult Bichon, since Bichons have small stomachs and won't be eating large meals.

- **Dog food** – Find out what your Bichon has been eating before buying new food. If you plan to change to a new food, only add 25% of the new food to the old food at first, slowly increasing the ratio of new food until the switch is complete. If your dog gets sick during this transition (diarrhea or vomiting), consult your vet for advice on choosing a new food.

- **Training treats** – Training treats are usually small, moist, soft, and tasty. They are used to motivate your training puppy or dog to follow commands and to use the potty in the proper location. Bichons are people pleasers and quick learners. And most of them are very food motivated. Having small treats on hand will really help the training process.

- **Distilled water** – Many Bichon owners swear by distilled water to help prevent pink or brown tear stains. This is not medically required, but worth trying if you are hoping to avoid fur staining around the eyes. This is not guaranteed to work, but many Bichon owners have claimed success by switching to distilled water.

Photo Courtesy of
Jennifer Powers

- **Chew toys** – If you are bringing home a puppy, look for toys that are designed for puppies and make sure they are size appropriate. Just because they are little, doesn't mean they can't chew through some sturdy toys. Senior dogs, or dogs with dental problems, may need a softer chew toy that won't damage their teeth further. Many rubber toys are rated according to the intensity of the chewer, making finding the right firmness achievable for most pet owners.

- **Bed** – When it comes to beds, bigger isn't always better. Bichons love to be snuggled into cozy settings and a smaller bed that makes them feel "hugged" will usually be preferred over a large bed (but not always!). Don't spend a lot of money on a bed until you learn your dog's bedding preferences. My Bichon will choose a pile of dirty laundry to sleep on any day, over a fancy bed.

- **Blankets** – Inexpensive, small fleece blankets are great purchases. New puppies, and even adult dogs, may have several accidents while settling in. Two to three small throw blankets will be great because you can throw them into the washing machine if they get soiled. And if they get chewed up or damaged, they are easier to throw away than an heirloom quilt.

- **Old towels** – Been thinking about getting some new bathroom towels? Great! Now you can save the old ones for your new Bichon who will likely give you plenty to clean up in the beginning. Towels also make great bedding, or can be laid over their dog bed to help keep it clean.

- **Pee pads** – Whether or not to use pee pads to train your Bichon is a personal preference. Pee pads can be purchased at a pet store or online, and can be placed in your dog's playpen, secluded room, or by the door they usually enter and exit to potty. With proper training, pee pads signal to your dog that this is where they should potty indoors.

- **Urine remover for carpets and upholstery** – Urine, and the smells it leaves, can be difficult to remove. Purchase an enzyme urine remover to help clean up urine, and hopefully remove the odor so your Bichon does not habitually return to the stain for repeated accidents.

- **Enclosures** – Pet gates, baby gates, playpens, play yards, and other enclosures will help keep your new dog safe, and your house more sanitary. These items can often be found used and be pretty inexpensive. Check online for great deals, or check out some yard sales.

- **Grooming supplies** – Grooming is covered in detail in chapter 15, but for now, at least have a metal dog comb and slicker brush on hand for basic grooming needs. Also, a small dog toothbrush would be great, to help your new dog get used to oral hygiene care.

- **Flea and tick prevention (if age appropriate)** – If you have an immediate vet appointment, you can wait and discuss this with your vet. If you are adopting an adult Bichon and have a favorite brand already, feel free to grab a box.

- **Medication** – If your dog is already on a prescription medication, make sure to pick it up when you pick up your dog. Find out how many doses are remaining so you can be sure to refill the prescription before it runs out.

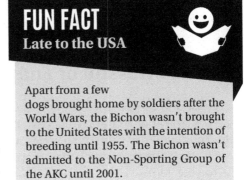

FUN FACT
Late to the USA

Apart from a few dogs brought home by soldiers after the World Wars, the Bichon wasn't brought to the United States with the intention of breeding until 1955. The Bichon wasn't admitted to the Non-Sporting Group of the AKC until 2001.

- **Clothing** – Okay, this might not be a necessity, but it sure can be a lot of fun to pick out cute outfits for a Bichon. With their bubbly and outgoing personalities, it's fun to watch them get adoration from strangers and neighbors alike. But on a serious note, if it is quite cold when you are bringing your new family member home, a jacket or sweater can really warm up your new pup, while they warm your heart!

As promised, here is your list of must haves and the cheapest ways to get them:

From your local thrift store (or in your linen closet):

- Blankets
- Towels
- Bedding
- Collars
- Leashes
- Bowls

Baby onesies (just cut off the bottom half), leg warmers (slide over and past the head and onto the body, and cut holes for the front legs to poke through) and other stretchy clothing items that you can cut to fit your dog to keep them warm.

From the shelter:

- Collars
- Leashes
- Bowls
- Food
- Treats

Ask them if you can get a month's supply of heart worm medicine and flea and tick prevention.

From the grocery store:

- White vinegar (for cleaning) – Dilute 10 to 1 with water and always test it in an inconspicuous area of fabric or carpet before using liberally, as vinegar can lighten anything made of fibers.
- Empty spray bottle for your vinegar solution
- Buy-one-get-one-free packages of food or treats

Week 1: Stressful or Fun?

Week one can set the tone for the weeks and months to follow. Having a plan may not guarantee success, but not having a plan certainly won't help. Your plan may turn into a series of contingency plans, and that's okay as well. But being proactive, rather than reactive, is wise when adding someone to your family. Here are some things you want to talk about, or think about, and devise a plan of action:

1. What kind of potty training are we going to try first? If that doesn't work, what is our backup plan?

2. Are we going to crate train? What is our goal with crate training? Where will we put the crate?

3. Where will the dog sleep? How will we ensure it is safe at night? Do I want a dog in my bed long term? Does my partner? Can my child handle the responsibility of sleeping with a pet?

4. Who will get up to take the dog outside during the night?

5. Who will clean up messes? Where will we put the waste? What products do we want to use?

6. Where will we keep the dog while we are away for work or errands?

7. What furniture may the dog be on, if at all?

8. What vaccines or medical care will it need when we get it?

9. What kind of training do we want to do? What has our research about training methodology led us to? What are the main things we want to teach our pet to do, or not do? How will we achieve this goal?

10. How will I socialize and acclimate my new dog in the first week? What is our plan if the pup is fearful, aggressive, withdrawn, or doesn't get along with my other pets?

Leave room to make changes if needed, but having a mindful and well thought out plan will make you feel more in control, thus increasing your confidence. Talking with your housemates or family and communicating the goals, rules, and expectations will help decrease confusion for the dog, and frustration for the humans. Following a plan will hopefully decrease your stress level, making your home warm and welcoming for the new addition. And a safe dog is a dog ready to learn new things.

The Ride Home

We discuss car travel at length in Chapter 13, but I'd like to add a few notes about picking up your Bichon and your first ride together. First of all, be prepared. Have a collar and a leash. Even if the photos of your new dog show it in a collar, it doesn't mean that the collar will go with the dog. If you don't have a collar and a leash, taking the puppy for a potty walk will likely not be possible.

Bichons are outgoing and playful, but they need a bit of time to get to know you. For this reason, expect your new dog to be a bit nervous. Bring someone with you to drive or hold the dog so you aren't distracted while driving. If you are going alone to get the dog, make sure to have a crate to put it in and line the crate with a pee pad or a towel, or both. Instead of being surprised if the dog has an accident, expect that it's possible and then you can celebrate if it doesn't. If it is a long drive, have several towels, pee pads, paper towels, disinfectant spray, and hand sanitizer. I would also bring a few small trash bags. Your new pup may not have an accident in the car close to civilization, but rather, it might have an accident 30 miles to the next gas station or fast food restaurant. Also have a way for your new dog to drink water if the drive is more than an hour.

The best policy when picking up your Bichon dog or puppy is to expect anything, prepare for most situations, and have a good sense of humor if it doesn't go your way. Try to stay relaxed and calm, and if you do have issues with your first car ride, be careful not to yell at your Bichon as they are extremely sensitive and can easily become fearful of anyone who yells and moves about in an agitated manner. And once a Bichon develops fear of someone, it can be months or even years for them to recover from this trauma, if they are able to fully recover from it. If you have children with you, explain the rules in advance. Make sure the kids are careful not to overwhelm your new dog, and if this is difficult to control, place your Bichon in a crate out of the reach of the children.

The First Day and Night at Home

"Be sure to have food, treats, and bedding ready to establish a comfortable place for them. Moving to a new home is always a big transition day. They may be a bit worried about the whole process."

Vicki Turner
Turner Dog Ranch

Similar to the ride home, your puppy or dog might be scared or just plain excited. There will be a lot of new smells and sights in your house and if it is a puppy it is likely the first night away from the home it was born in. It might take a while for your dog to settle down. Just make sure the dog is someplace quiet and comfortable. If the foster home or breeder gives you a blanket or toy they like, keep that with them so they have a familiar scent to comfort them.

Photo Courtesy of Sally Wegher

When you arrive at home, the first thing you will want to do is take your dog to potty. Take your time with this. It may take 10-15 minutes or more, to get your new dog to pee or poop. When it happens, give lots of praise and a small treat. A successful potty experience and celebration is an excellent way to start your relationship with your Bichon, signaling to him/her clear expectations.

Once inside, take your new dog room by room on a leash; this way they can sniff everything and you can quickly move them outside if they begin to potty or mark in your home. If they do potty or mark, tell them no and take them back outside. Clean up the mess without a fuss.

If you have other pets who accept new friends easily, introduce them and let them sniff each other. If you have a pet that is irritable or aggressive, take appropriate precautions and use a leash to keep control of the dog in question and enlist help if you are worried about how the introduction will go. After you introduce the dogs, do not leave them unattended. They are still learning each other's boundaries, and can easily cross them without intending to. They will need your guidance and leadership. Your presence will help them both feel safe. Make sure that there aren't toys, bones, or food sitting out that might cause a ruckus between animals.

Be mindful that jealousy between pets is possible. Be careful not to ignore one of your pets, as they can become sensitive to it. Some dogs guard their resources, and you are a very valuable resource to your pet. Also be aware that even though Bichons typically get along with most other dogs, they can become jealous as well, and may try to nip at another animal that could be much bigger. In this regard, some Bichons bite off more than they can chew. Protect all your pets but make sure that you don't reward or ignore jealous behavior that could lead to aggression.

Show your dog their food and water bowl. Encourage them to drink water. See if they are interested in food. Monitor their eating style and behaviors while eating. If you have other pets, do this with your other pets in another room or outside. If you plan to feed them near each other, keep their food on opposite ends of the room until you know what to expect. If there aren't any signs of food (or even water) aggression, you can gradually move their bowls closer together. After eating, take them to potty again.

When you first get your Bichon home, you should take them out every hour to ninety minutes. Your goal here is to catch your dog doing more things right than it does wrong to build its confidence and enthusiasm in the training process.

When it is time to go to bed, stick to the plan that you have created even if you feel pangs of guilt for not allowing them to do things like sleep in your bed. You made these decisions, either alone or as a team with sober thinking, which is more likely to reflect your true desires and what is likely best for your household in the long run. And unless you live alone, it is important to value the preferences of the other people you live with.

If you are allowing the new dog in the bed with you, make sure you have a way to keep it safe from falling off of the bed. You might want to put extra pillows and fluffy blankets on the floor around your bed as a safety net in case the little guy or girl takes a spill.

If you are crate training, or confining the dog to a space outside of your room, you will need to choose a location that fits the rest of your game plan. If your dog is too young to hold its potty all night, you will need to keep it close to you so you can hear it announce its potty needs. Conversely, you can put the crate (or confinement) far enough away so you don't hear it cry or bark. If you choose to do this, you will need to set an alarm or timer to get up to check on it and/or let it out to potty. Young dogs cannot hold their potty for long, so don't expect them to do so. Plan accordingly so your new addition knows it can count on you to meet its needs.

When you get up the next morning, check the entire area (in your room, the crate, or whatever room the dog slept in) for any potty accidents. Pull out the dog's bedding from the crate and look at it, feel it, and smell it. Sometimes dogs will hide their accidents, or the urine will simply settle to the bottom of the stack, and you will find a stinky, nasty mess later. Even worse, your dog will have gotten used to peeing or pooping in its crate and then lying in its mess. This is the last thing you want to do, as creating a happy, healthy, and clean pet who desires to be clean is of primary importance for happy pet ownership.

Choosing a Vet

Choosing a vet doesn't have to be complicated. If you live in a rural area, you might choose to use the only vet in town. If you have several choices where you live, look at options close to your home. Also look for vets that have some weekend hours. Also, some vet clinics have "sister clinics" in town that share the same database, so they would have your pet's records if the clinic you normally use is closed. Having multiple options is good when they have complementary hours, thus helping you avoid having to use an after-hours emergency clinic.

Here are some other factors to consider when choosing a vet:

- What kind of reviews do they have?
- What do your friends have to say about the clinic?
- Is the waiting room comfortable?
- What are their wait times like?
- Do they require an appointment?
- Do they have an on-call doctor all the time? How do their emergency rates compare to their standard rates?
- What procedures do they not offer at the clinic?
- Do they do basic bloodwork in-house?
- Do they read X-rays the same day or do they have them sent out? How long will results take?
- Can you access your pet's records online or from a phone app?
- Do they offer boarding (if you prefer to use a vet for boarding rather than a boarding facility or care in your home)?
- Do they offer grooming?
- If you embrace alternative health care approaches, how does this vet feel about them? Will they support you in your desires to treat in holistic ways when appropriate?
- How do you feel when you are in the clinic? How does your Bichon feel?

Before choosing a vet, call and ask to schedule a courtesy visit, also known as a "happy visit." This will allow you to meet the staff and doctors, check out the facility, and get a feel for wait times and the general flow of appointments there. You can see how they treat you and your dog and see how your dog reacts to the environment. If you have major concerns with your first visit, keep looking until you find a vet that you love.

The First Vet Visit

Choosing a vet that you really like will help make the first official visit to the vet a lot easier; both you and your pet will know what to expect and hopefully you are both feeling relaxed.

Before scheduling your first visit, collect the records for your dog's previous visits and vaccines. When you call to schedule the visit, have these records or notes on hand in case the scheduler would like this information in advance. They will likely want to know where your pup is in the vaccination process.

Before your first visit, make notes about any concerns you have, any questions or have, and any observations that might concern the vet. Pay attention to how your pup is doing with eating, potty training, sleep training, basic obedience training, and any potential health concerns.

At the first visit, your vet will have you fill out some basic paperwork about your Bichon. Then they will take your dog's weight and take you both to an examination room. The vet tech or vet assistant will probably ask you basic questions about your dog, including what kind of food they are eating, potty training, health concerns, etc. They will also discuss with you the vaccines that your pup will be receiving that day.

Vaccines will be drawn according to your pet's weight and they may give the vaccines with you holding your pet, or more likely, the vet tech and the vet will do this together. They will probably take the pup's rectal temperature and may take a fecal sample. To avoid them having to do this invasively, you can bring a small stool sample from the yard or potty pad. Make sure the sample is fresh.

The vet will talk with you to address all of your concerns and they will give you a copy of all of the vaccines and tests done at the visit. Some clinics will give you a binder to keep all of your records. If they don't, I recommend getting a one-inch binder and keeping your records yourself. You will want to keep a copy of all documents they send home to you. Conversely, you can scan them, or take a photo, and upload them to your computer or wherever you keep an online version of important records.

Also, many vets have their own smartphone applications. If so, download the app and create an account while you are still at the vet (in case you have any trouble). Ask them the benefits of the app, which may include scheduling appointments, requesting refills, accessing records, or communicating concerns with your vet. There may be financial incentives to using the app, such as collecting points for exams or purchases, which may give you free or discounted purchases in the future.

Before leaving the visit, ask if you can go ahead and schedule your next visit for the next series of shots. If you don't need a visit for six months to a year, you can still go ahead and schedule an appointment. Even if you have to change the day and time of the appointment as it gets closer, you have taken the necessary steps to ensure that you don't forget altogether. More than likely, your clinic will send you a reminder either way, but being proactive puts you in the driver's seat and you are less likely to get behind on vaccines if you plan ahead.

Puppy and Obedience Classes

It is very important to take your dog to puppy or obedience classes, or to use a tried and true method for training them at home. Some Humane Societies will offer classes for an affordable rate. Also, there are dog daycares, training centers, or pet stores that offer classes as well. Lastly, you may consider a "board and train" option wherein you take your puppy or dog to a reputable training facility that will keep your dog for two weeks or more, working with them on the desired skills. Even if you have trained a dog before, going to a puppy or obedience class is an important socializing and bonding experience for you and your dog. Setting aside time each day and attending classes to focus on your dog or puppy will be hugely important to creating a lasting bond.

Here is some training that your puppy or dog may need, and hopefully receive:

- Basic Obedience:
  - Sit
  - Down (lying down)
  - Off (getting off of the furniture, or off of a person)
  - Leave It (leave it alone; don't touch)
  - Drop It (release it)
  - Stay
  - Come
  - Heel
  - Fetch
- Potty Training *tell me w/*
- Crate Training *place*
- Leash and Walk Training
- Bite Inhibition Training
- No Jump
- No Bark Training
- Threshold Training (teaching your dog to wait before walking through a door)
- Recall Training

48

It's important to note that even though your Bichon will always be pretty small, that doesn't mean that you can ignore training, like teaching them not to jump on you or nip at people. Even though they are small, that doesn't mean that they are harmless, and I can assure you that your family and friends will enjoy being around your Bichon a lot more if they aren't getting mud on their clothes or getting nail or bite scratches. Bad behavior is bad behavior, no matter how cute the offender.

If you are training your dog at home, I would encourage you to learn the common hand signals for basic commands. You might be surprised at how many dogs learn these hand signals, and how well they respond to them, even if they have never been taught them. In my dog business, I use a common hand signal for "sit" and I am always impressed at how many dogs I have just met acknowledge and obey the hand signal.

You may or may not choose to teach your Bichon tricks. It's certainly not a requirement, but Bichons are smart and active dogs. They are often treat motivated, and almost always affection motivated, so teaching your Bichon tricks will likely be highly rewarding for both of you.

Perhaps one of the most important reasons for teaching obedience is the aspect of socialization. Young puppies benefit greatly from being socialized. Just being around new dogs, new people, and new places (especially in a safe setting), will help prepare your dog for a lifetime of friendships and the emotional flexibility to try new situations with little to no fear or anxiety. Training is way more than just being in control. It is about teaching your dog what is safe and not safe, teaching it that there is a world full of relationships and experiences to enjoy, and teaching your pup how to appropriately fit into its world.

CHAPTER 5
Being a Puppy Parent

"Bichons are very friendly and like to be with you at all times. They quickly make friends with everyone they meet."

Betsy Savage
Dazzling Bichons

Standing By Your Own Expectations

It is important to do research and set expectations for your new puppy or dog. Puppies and Bichons of any age are adorable and can easily break any willpower you might have just by looking at you. However, it is important that if you set expectations for your Bichon that you stand by them, no matter how persuasive their puppy dog eyes are. For instance, if you decide you do not want the puppy on furniture or to sleep in bed with you or your family members, then hold fast to keeping the puppy off of the furniture. Don't hold it while you are sitting on the couch or in bed because then it will think it is okay. If you want the puppy to be crate trained and it is whining a lot at night in its crate, don't cave and bring it to bed with you; this will make the training even tougher. These are decisions that should be made prior to getting the puppy. It is important for the entire family to be aware of them so the puppy doesn't get confused. Bichons specifically love to please the ones they love, so allowing them to do something that you do not want them to do and then scolding them later is confusing and unfair.

Just like anything that is adorable, fluffy, and snuggly, standing by your expectations is much easier said than done. It is also important to go with the flow to some degree. Living with a puppy (or a new dog) is chaotic and things will not go perfectly according to plan. Don't set too many restrictions for yourself or your puppy, but also stick to the plan when it comes to what is best for your household in the long run. Also know that training is a process. Probably number one on your list is that the dog does not go to the bathroom in the house; however, that takes time. Patience and encouragement will be needed to properly train your pup.

Photo Courtesy of Lorry Weiss

How to Crate Train

Crate training is very popular and safe for your puppy. All of my dogs have been crate trained. We rescued my current dog when she was one year old. The rescue we got her from had crate trained her, which was awesome. We upheld the crate training for about six months to help with her transition to our home and until we knew her temperament very well. Then we left the crate open so she could go in there voluntarily. Some people choose to use the crate throughout their dog's entire life, which is completely okay; however, it is unique to each family and each dog. Some people use the crate at night but not during the day or vice versa.

Before you begin the crate training process, you must first make sure the crate is a safe and comfortable space for your dog. Never use it as a punishment to your dog. Second, and possibly most importantly, make sure your dog or puppy is not in the crate for too long, especially in the beginning. This is critical. Your puppy or adult Bichon must always feel fully confident that you are coming back and that they are safe and comfortable in the meantime. Bichons have small bladders, and puppies are even more challenged at holding their bladder. If you expect more than they are capable of, you will leave them potentially anxious or upset. You must give them ample opportunity to succeed and to do this you will have to be reasonable in your expectations of them.

Third, be aware of your dog's health while in the crate. This is especially important for Bichons who tend to have separation anxiety. If the crate is causing them too much anxiety or they are at risk for injuring themselves trying to get out (by biting or scratching the crate, causing dental or nail damage), it might be worth looking into another option such as room confinement or the use of baby gates. You might also consider hiring a dog walker for midday breaks if you will be gone longer than your dog can comfortably and realistically handle.

Choosing the Crate

It is very important to choose the correct crate for your dog. Size is the most important factor. Your dog should be able to stand up and turn around in it. If you have a puppy who will continue to grow, you can buy a crate that will fit it at full size, and put a divider in to make it smaller. As your puppy grows you can move the divider back until it is big enough for the crate. There are several types of crates including plastic, cloth, and metal.

Photo Courtesy of
Marija Deakulovic

Photo Courtesy of
Kassandra Paull

The type of crate you choose is based on your preference; however, getting the correct size is most important.

In addition to your pup being able to stand, stretch, and turn around, there should also be room for a small bed or blanket (or a towel) for them to sleep on. You will also need to make sure there's enough room for food and water either on the floor, or clipped to the crate itself. Using clipped bowls could prevent spills, especially with water. I prefer to use clipped bowls in the sides of the crate instead of on the door because dogs tend to focus their "pawing" efforts on the door and might knock the bolts out of the clips.

Conversely, it's important while the dog or puppy is training that the crate not be too large. A crate that is too spacious will give your training pooch enough area to find a spot to potty. By keeping the space cozy and intimate, your dog will hopefully choose clean and dry over wet or soiled and will hopefully work harder to refrain from going potty in the crate.

Introducing Your Bichon Frise to the Crate

In order for the puppy to feel at home and safe in the crate, it must go into the crate willingly and in a relaxed manner. Some puppies take to their crate very quickly, while others require a bit more time and patience. It is important to go at the pace of the puppy or dog and take small steps throughout the training process. The first step is to introduce your puppy to the crate. Make sure there is a blanket or bed in the crate for your puppy so it looks comfortable. To start, put the crate in part of the house you will be in a lot. It could be the kitchen, living room, or any other area where you and your family spend a lot of time.

Take the door off the crate and leave it open. Some dogs have a natural curiosity and will check it out. Others might show absolutely no interest in the crate. In order to encourage their interest, you could sit by the crate and call them over or play with them near the crate. You could also give your puppy some of their favorite treats, first outside the crate then put the treats into the crate. If your puppy has a favorite toy, you could toss the toy into the crate so they follow it. Take the time your dog needs to be comfortable in the crate.

When they go into the crate, let them relax. You might also offer your pup a treat when it goes in, but then casually walk away. We want our Bichons to naturally associate their crates with positives like treats, comfort, and love.

Getting Your Puppy or Dog Used to Spending Time in the Crate

Remember that crate training your puppy or dogs could take two weeks or it might take two months. It really depends on how your puppy takes to their crate and on how consistent you are with the "rules." Once your pup is comfortable going in and out of the crate, start feeding it meals in there. It is important to go at the speed that your pup is comfortable. When it will eat its food in the crate comfortably, then close the door while the puppy is eating but open it right away. Once it is comfortable with that, leave the door closed for five minutes after your puppy is done eating. Slowly lengthen the amount of time. The idea is to do it slow enough so your puppy doesn't start whining. If this does happen, then return to the time frame where the puppy did not whine and go more slowly. Some pups will not need this slow a pace, but it's a good rule of thumb for dogs who are learning the crate for the first time, or for those who have had less than ideal crate experiences in the past.

When your puppy is comfortable with meals and short periods of time in the crate, then keep expanding the time frame. It is important to be consistent. You should have a command such as "crate" or "kennel" which you say every time you want your puppy to enter the crate. If you have a treat, they will likely pick up on the command much quicker. As you leave your puppy in the crate for longer periods of time, spend time near the crate and away from it.

For example, you could try for ten minutes. The first three minutes sit near the crate. Don't interact with your puppy, just sit there quietly. Then leave the room for four or five minutes. Try not to make a lot of noise around the house that would make your puppy want to leave the crate. Then come back and sit near the crate for the final two to three minutes. Praise your puppy for good behavior and not whining.

Work your way up to about thirty minutes with your puppy in the crate where you are out of the room more than you are in it. Once your puppy can do this successfully, you could try leaving for a short errand like getting gas or picking up your kids from school. Don't leave food or water in the crate as it will make them have to go to the bathroom, unless they have already mastered this period of time without pottying in their crate. You can leave one or a few toys in the crate though to keep your puppy entertained. Just make sure the toys are safe and not a choking hazard. If your Bichon can break off pieces of the toy by chewing on it, then it is hazardous.

The key is to try and keep your pup from whining or associating the crate with a negative experience. Try to make it fun and relaxing for your pup. If you want to crate them at night that is the next step in training. When you start crating them at night, make sure you keep the crate near you so the puppy doesn't feel isolated. If you want them somewhere else, wait until they sleep through the night before moving the crate somewhere else.

Crate training can be time-consuming and might even be frustrating, but it can be a great option for your puppy, especially if you desire to keep your pup, and your house, safe while you are away.

Bedtime

Bedtime can be tough, especially for puppies. They usually cannot go an entire night without going to the bathroom. While it is important to meet all of their needs, they also need to learn how to sleep through the night.

When preparing your puppy (or new dog) for bed, a routine is essential. They come to know the routine and it can help settle them down as they grow. It is important to take your Bichon for a walk or have play time a couple hours before you actually want them to sleep. This gives them time to settle down after an exciting time. If you play with your pup right before bed, they might want to continue playing and elongate the process.

Your pup might also respond well to calming music. Classical music is recommended, but not required as most dogs will be calmed by any reasonably calm music. Not only can the sound calm down your Bichon, it also will mask any sounds that might be distracting or trigger your Bichon like a car going by or something outside.

Keeping some of their favorite items including blankets or beds in the crate can help them calm down. Make sure not to put a favorite toy in the crate because they might associate that with playtime. Also, if you are working on crate training your dog, make sure you keep to your training. The crate can be a great tool for teaching your puppy to sleep through the night and how to calm down before bedtime. When they are young, keep the crate near your bed so you can hear them if they have to go out. There is a high likelihood that your puppy will need to go out in the middle of the night. If this happens, make sure the bathroom break is all business. Make it as boring as possible and don't engage if the puppy thinks it is play time. This means no cuddles or conversation. But it's definitely essential to praise them for going to the bathroom outside.

Chewing

It's natural for dogs to chew, especially when they are teething. While chewing itself is just part of being a dog at any age and is not inherently bad, the chewing should be focused on toys or dog-safe bones, not your clothes, shoes, furniture, or even your carpet or walls. Puppies, in particular, can be quite destructive and might even hurt themselves if they like to chew on cords or plastic. It can also get expensive if they chew on clothes, shoes, or furniture.

Knowing that your puppy will chew, try to keep possible items of interest out of their reach. Try to put shoes away in a closet, keep your clothes off the floor. If you have kids, be aware of the puppy getting ahold of their toys. It's unreasonable to expect your dog to know what is a toy and what is not, until they are taught. Even once they know, some items will be a strong temptation for the rest of their lives.

The most important thing is to be attentive to your puppy or adult (training) dog at all times. This can be nearly impossible, but if they are out and romping around then there is the potential for them to eat or ingest something. When you leave the house, this is where crate training is beneficial. Then the puppy is contained with safe toys and you do not have to worry about them harming themselves or your belongings.

A lot of times chewing can be a sign of boredom or even anxiety (unless it's a young puppy, who is just naturally going to chew everything). If your adult dog or older puppy is chewing everything in sight, more exercise could offer mental stimulation. You can also get puzzle toys for your dog to keep them busy while you are gone.

If you find your dog or puppy chewing on something they shouldn't be, the first thing you should do is interrupt what they are doing. Do something to distract them away from what they are chewing on. Then give them a toy that is okay for them to chew on. When they start chewing on the appropriate toy, give them verbal praise and physical affection.

Be very consistent about interrupting and distracting your puppy. Bichons are very receptive to positive reinforcement but can also be pretty stubborn. As frustrated as you might get, remain positive but firm with your pup. Training is not an instantaneous thing and your pup might continuously find other things to chew on. Be sure to provide a variety of age-appropriate toys for your puppy or dog.

Growling and Barking

If your puppy or dog is growling because it is scared, you will definitely know. It will be very tense and genuinely look scared. Bichons are not very good at hiding their emotions, so use this to your advantage. In the case that your pup is scared, be sure to deescalate the situation as fast as possible. The most important thing to do is to stop whatever you (or someone else) are doing that is agitating the puppy immediately. From there you can problem solve to determine why and how the pup got agitated and make needed adjustments. For example, my Bichon can be jumpy with loud and sudden movements or noises, so we have tried to be a little more aware of our "bull in a china shop" movements around our pup.

More likely, your puppy is growling while it is exploring its surroundings. If you do not want your puppy to growl while playing, just stop the game until it calms down, then continue playing. Your puppy will learn to associate growling with stopping the game. But remember to look for signs of fearfulness like a dropped or tucked tail, sudden barking, or aggressive posture. A really scared dog may even pee or poop suddenly. It's important to learn the difference between playful and scared/aggressive growling or barking in your Bichon.

Puppies generally won't bite out of anger but nip when they get excited or are playing very intensely. This is completely normal and you should follow the same procedure as above: stop playing when they bite or nip. Once they calm down you can start playing again. Don't yell at them. Instead, reinforce good behavior.

A NOTE FROM RACHEL:

My dog right now is a very loud player. We adopted her when she was an adult, and her growling when she played was a bit startling at first, but then we realized she just played loud. One of my closest friends also has a dog that plays loud and when they get together it almost sounds like they are fighting, but they are having a blast! It is important to know your dog and their tendencies. I know if my dog is growling because she is agitated or if she is just having a good time. Keep this in mind as you get to know your puppy and as they grow up.

Digging

If you have a garden or a yard, be aware that your Bichon might dig. Bichons in general don't tend to dig but it is not unheard of. Bichons usually get into mischief in other ways, like running away when you call them, getting on the table or counter, getting into the trash, or using your dishwasher full of dirty dishes as a "Bichon buffet."

A lot of times a dog will dig out of boredom or separation anxiety. If this is the case, dedicate more time to playing with your puppy. This could include one on one play time, going for walks, or going to a dog park. Puppies are very curious and need a lot of different outlets for their energy. They also just want to be with you so giving them a lot of love and affection is important. Once they begin barking in the yard, they are probably ready to come in. By letting them back inside when you recognize they are bored or lonely, you will decrease the likelihood that they will become destructive.

Dogs also dig to control their body temperature. Be aware of the temperature outside. If it is warm, make sure there is a cool, shaded area for your dog to lay down. Also make sure you provide plenty of water. On the other hand, if it is cold, then provide an insulated or warm area for your dog.

Leaving Your Puppy Home Alone and Separation Anxiety

"Bichons really do not like being alone and in order to be their happiest they need to be with people, or other dogs, most of the time."

Jeanette Neagu
Takoda Dogs

Leaving your puppy home alone can be tough. They are adorable and you will want to give them all of your attention and time, but you probably have a job or other responsibilities. Unfortunately, you can't just stay home and snuggle and play with your puppy all of the time. It is highly encouraged that you crate train your puppy. This is the easiest way to ensure they are safe and comfortable when you are away from home.

It is important to take into consideration the age and needs of your puppy. If you get a young puppy, they might not be able to go a full workday without going to the bathroom. You might want to consider stopping home

*Photo Courtesy of
Tammy Capozzoli*

during lunch or hiring a dog walker to ensure your puppy is taken care of during the day.

If you don't want to crate train, another option is to leave them in a restricted area such as the kitchen. Until your puppy is completely comfortable in your house and you are confident they will not harm any of your stuff or themselves while you are gone, it is good to start small like a crate or confined area. One of the keys to leaving your puppy home alone is to get them used to alone time. Start with leaving them alone in the crate or area while you are there. This way you have some control over their reaction.

Bichons are very well known for getting extremely attached to their families. There is a pretty high likelihood that your puppy might develop separation anxiety, despite what you do to prevent it. Some signs of separation anxiety could include whining, barking, defecating, urinating, or destroying property. But separation anxiety should not rule your life or your pup's.

There are a few tips for preventing separation anxiety with your puppy or adult Bichon. Bichons tend to love new activities, treats, and puzzles. If they are crate trained, put them in their crate for 10 or 15 minutes at random times with their favorite toy or treat to get them used to the concept of your coming and going. Only give them their special toy or treat when they spend time in the crate though. If they associate the crate with their favorite toy or special treats, then they will want to go in the crate to receive their favorite toy or treat. Always keep crating, or anything that separates you from your Bichon, positive and "matter of fact."

Here are some tried and true tips for helping to prevent or manage separation anxiety in your Bichon:

- **Have a positive and relaxed demeanor.** Nervous dog parents tend to have nervous dogs, and Bichons are particularly aware of their owner's emotions. It's best to look at the "event" of leaving as a non-issue. Check your emotions and remember that it is more kind to your pup to be strong and calm than it is to get worked up emotionally.

- **Leave a human-scented item behind.** Dogs, especially Bichons, love to lie on their owner's unwashed clothes as it makes them feel more secure. A shirt, sweater, or bathrobe works great for this.

- **Be predictable.** Use the same methodology and the same language each time you leave. Say things like, "I love you. See you soon!" And use the same excited energy when you return.

- **Don't linger.** Leaving your Bichon at home for a spell shouldn't resemble an airport goodbye scene from a movie. Just keep your goodbyes short and sweet and your Bichon will likely adopt your chipper attitude. Even if they don't stay completely calm, increasing their nervous or anxious energy will not help them at all.

- **Use monotonous sounds to calm them.** A fan, radio, CD, streaming device, TV, or white noise machine are all great options to create a steady sound in the background that is usually reassuring for Bichons. Play around with different sounds to see if they have a favorite.

- **Provide a chew toy.** Give them something safe to chew on. Chewing helps to physically reduce anxiety in dogs.

- **Cover their crate.** Not all dogs will like to have their crate covered, but for some, this simple act will make a huge difference in helping them to feel secure.

- **Use calming essential oils like lavender.** You can put 2-3 drops on their blanket or collar or rub 1-2 drops into your hands and massage it lightly into their hair.

- **Exercise them before leaving.** A tired dog is usually a calm dog, and Bichons have a surprising amount of energy for their size. Don't have time for a walk? Try throwing a tennis ball in the house and let them chase it for 5-10 minutes. They will enjoy this special time and may not mind too much that you have to run out for a bit.

- **Make your reunions simple and sweet.** When you get home, enjoy snuggling your baby, but remember coming and going is part of life, so don't feel the need to go overboard with the celebration every time.

- **Get another Bichon!** Dogs who have sleeping companions tend to be more relaxed.

If your Bichon is particularly upset when you leave, consider working with a trainer or contacting your dog's vet to discuss calming treats, CBD oil, or prescription anxiety medications. Meds should not be the go-to method for treating anxiety, but if your Bichon is in danger of hurting itself or becomes destructive when left alone, then meds can help bridge the gap while you help to train and reassure your Bichon to be calm when alone. Your confidence is your secret weapon when training your Bichon to trust the process. If they can tell that leaving home gives you anxiety, they are extremely likely to become stressed too. But if your words, body language, tone of voice, and actions tell them that everything will be okay, they will more than likely believe you.

A NOTE FROM KRIS:

As a boarding professional, I occasionally meet dog owners who seem let down that their dogs don't show extreme signs of separation anxiety, as it seems that some dog owners feel that their dog's anxiety is proof of their bond. But let me assure you that the dogs who have a strong and healthy attachment with their owners have learned to enjoy themselves with or without their owners. It should be our goal as pet owners to give our dogs the gift of being highly adaptable and feeling safe to enjoy time away from their owners or home. I promise your Bichon will be happy to see you when you get back, even if they don't show it when you leave.

Running Away

Sometimes your Bichon's curiosity might get the better of him. Dogs don't usually run away because they don't love you but because they see or smell something, follow it, and get lost. Also, sometimes they just like to explore, or may have a favorite potty spot outside of the approved zone. Bichons are very curious and active dogs so be aware that this is a genuine risk and you should take all precautions to keep them from running away from you and into potential danger.

Here are some practical tips for preventing your Bichon from running away:

- Make sure to train your humans to close gates and doors.
- Use a baby gate or playpen to separate your Bichon from the door before opening it (if there isn't a fence outside that door).

- Teach your Bichon threshold training, meaning that they do not go through doors without your permission. However, do not rely solely on threshold training, especially if you live near busy roads.

- Pick up and hold your Bichon before opening the door.

- Put signs on your doors and gates that let people know not to open the door. Sometimes family friends might let themselves in, not realizing that there is a tiny white risk taker ready to take advantage of any opportunity to take a neighborhood romp.

The most common reason a Bichon might run from you is that they think you are playing, or that they are hoping you will take their hint for a walk. If they think you are playing, if you try to chase after them, they will probably keep running. A good trick of the trade is to call your Bichon's name in a very excited voice and then start jogging in the opposite direction. This should catch your puppy's attention and in theory they will follow you to continue the game. If you have a ball, try throwing it in the direction you would like them to go.

When looking for a dog that has gotten away from you, take some flavorful treats (bacon, hot dogs, lunchmeat, cheese, or whatever is handy) with you and when you are near your dog, crouch down and offer the treats while speaking in a high-pitched and playful voice. Another trick is to get in your car and when you get near them, open the car door and ask if they want to go for a ride. Usually they will hop right in. If all else fails, walk around with another friendly dog while you look for your Bichon. Your Bichon will probably be excited to see their friend. Make sure you have an extra leash with you to put on the pup to make getting back home more manageable if you are walking.

HELPFUL TIP
Vaccination Sensitivity

Bichons are more sensitive to vaccinations than many other breeds, so it's important to keep an eye on your Bichon for several hours after it gets shots to look out for signs of an allergic reaction such as hives, lethargy, soreness, or facial swelling. In rare cases, allergic reactions to vaccines can be fatal to Bichons.

As you go through training with your Bichon, you can work to teach them a command to stop them when they run away. An effective one is to have them lie down where they are and then you go to them. You can ask your instructor about how to properly train your dog to respond to a recall word or sound.

Remember, unless your Bichon is very well trained, you should not be walking them off leash in an open area. A dog park is a great place for your puppy to be off leash in a (usually) safe environment. Make sure your puppy has updated tags and a microchip so if someone finds them then they can contact you. Additionally, make sure your Bichon is socialized well and is comfortable with meeting new people or dogs. That way if they run away and you cannot find them, they might be comfortable approaching someone.

The important takeaway is to reward your puppy for coming back to you, not punish him or her. If your puppy associates coming back with a punishment then this could scare them from coming back. Love on them, praise them, offer them treats, and do whatever it takes to be clear that you are happy to have them back.

A NOTE FROM RACHEL:

When I was growing up my Bichon, Buddy, loved going on walks. In fact he loved them so much that he would tag along on other dogs' walks. We had an electric fence, but sometimes the squirrels would chew through the line. People in our neighborhood knew Buddy and sometimes let him walk around the block with them before bringing him home!

A NOTE FROM KRIS:

We live on 17 acres and have a walking trail that connects to even more acreage. I am able to walk Ricky without a leash on our property. He has never tried to run away, but will run a bit into the woods to explore. When I call him back, he comes to me for praise and to be petted. Because he is such a good listener, he can be off leash, and walks are a lot of fun for both of us.

CHAPTER 6
Housetraining

Let's start this chapter with a warning: Bichons are notoriously bad at learning not to go to the bathroom in the house, which is usually attributed to their stubbornness. Even though Bichons can be stubborn and challenging to train, they love making you happy. They also do not respond well to negative reinforcement, so it is important to stay patient and positive even if it takes longer than normal to train your puppy or dog.

The First Few Weeks

Whether you are bringing home an adult dog or a young puppy, you will likely have to work with it on housetraining. Being in a new environment will cause a disruption in your dog's routine so even mature adult dogs who are housetrained might have some accidents as they adjust to their new home and routine.

The first few weeks are critical for your new family member. Work to establish a routine that works for both you and the dog. The routine will probably change over time as your dog matures and you get used to each other, but for the first few weeks with your dog, try to stay as consistent as possible. Feed the dog at the same time every day and don't leave food out between meals, especially with a puppy who might not have control over their bowels quite yet.

Take a puppy outside every half hour. This way it should never have to wait to go to the bathroom. When it successfully goes to the bathroom outside, give a lot of praise and positive reinforcement. Usually by 16 to 20 weeks old, your puppy should have fairly good control of his bladder. If he is successfully eliminating without accidents then push back the amount of time you wait before taking him out. This could be a long process, but will be worth it in the end.

When your pup has accidents, take it outside and then clean up the messes quickly and thoroughly. Pick up solid feces with toilet paper and flush them down the toilet. Clean up loose stools and urine with paper towels and cleaner made specifically for pet accidents. Look for a cleaner containing enzymes that is designed to completely eliminate the odor of the accident, decreasing the likelihood that the pup will continue to return to the same spot for accidents.

Luckily, adult dogs should catch on fairly quick. They are likely at least partially housetrained if you rescued them and will simply need to get acquainted with their new environment and routine. For some dogs, you may have to do very little training, others could take some more encouragement and patience, as some dogs were given to the shelter because of potty training issues. However, it is important to remember that all dogs are trainable given the time and safe space to achieve the goals presented to them.

Photo Courtesy of Michelle McKenna

Crate Training for Housetraining Use

Crate training can be an extremely valuable tool to use, especially when you first get your puppy. It helps teach them routine, discipline, and how to be alone. Crate training was covered in detail in Chapter 5 but let's now apply it specifically to housetraining.

As discussed in Chapter 5, don't use the crate for punishment; instead, make it a fun and welcoming place for your puppy to hang out, relax, and sleep.

Dogs tend not to like to sleep where they have gone to the bathroom, so crating your puppy at night could encourage him or her to wake you up when they have to go out instead of having an accident. Also, if they do have an accident, you know exactly where it is and won't find any surprises throughout your house.

Crate training for housetraining can come in handy, especially at night. When you first bring your puppy home he will likely have to go out every 30 minutes or so. When he is in the crate you can teach him to get your attention by making a habit of taking him outside when he seeks your attention through barking, whining, or other attention-getting activities and rewarding him for his successful potties outside. Gradually work on lengthening the time between potty breaks. Also, you can work on teaching that outside is a place to do their business, not necessarily to immediately play. With positive reinforcement and a clear routine, your Bichon Frise should catch on quickly and the process of housetraining will go smoothly.

Photo Courtesy of
Michael Tortorete

Playpens and Doggy Doors

You may not want to crate train your puppy, and that is completely fine; however, it is not necessarily wise to give your puppy full run of the house as soon as you bring him home. Even with a full-grown dog, adjusting to a new space can be hard. Using a playpen can be a great alternative to a crate as it is still a confined area but can be made larger than a crate. Using baby gates to close off areas of your home or keep your dog in an area is another great option. The playpen could be on a hard floor surface for easy clean-up if there are accidents. You can put blankets and beds for your dog or puppy on the ground as well.

When picking out a playpen just make sure to get a dog-friendly one where your pup can't get stuck in between slats or otherwise injure himself. A playpen gives you a bit more flexibility with space and such, but it does not give your dog a home base or "bedroom" like a crate might. The same training techniques can be used with a playpen as with the crate.

A doggy door can be a good option as well. Just remember that the doggy door does not stop other pets from getting out or unwanted animals from getting into your house. To train your puppy to use a doggy door, start with the flap off of the doggy door so it can get used to going in and out without having to push the flap. Also make sure that you plan your doggy door for the full size your dog will get, not the size it is as a puppy. When you first get your puppy, he might be a bit too small to go through the doggy door unaided, but you can still start the training process.

You can train your puppy to go through the doggy door the exact same way you taught him or her to go into a crate in Chapter 5. Always use a lot of positive reinforcement and remember that items like doggy doors and crates aren't necessarily intuitive to your dog. He needs to be taught how to use them. Be a guide for your dog and offer a lot of treats and praise. You will have to teach your dog the difference between outside and inside as well. This should be a bit more intuitive to your dog or puppy but follow the housetraining practices above to make sure they understand.

HELPFUL TIP
Crate Training

While many people balk at the idea of keeping their dog in a crate, the reality is that your dog will likely be faced with a kennel at some point in its future, whether it's at the groomer, the vet, or in a carrier on a plane with you. You should crate train your Bichon puppy while house-training so it can feel comfortable in a crate in the future, even if you don't plan on keeping your pup in one on a regular basis.

Housetraining your puppy might be a challenge, but is completely possible. Their love of playing and all of the new sights and smells might make it hard for them to focus on going to the bathroom once they get outside. Stay patient, use all of the tools you have, and be a positive but consistent force in your puppy's life to help them become housetrained as quickly as possible.

A NOTE FROM KRIS:

My Bichon Ricky is a rescue and was close to a year old when I adopted him. He had some accidents when he came home with me but the frequency of those accidents decreased quickly. Ricky still has accidents from time to time, but it is usually connected to the weather. He resists going out in heavy rain. He does not mind getting his paws wet like some Bichons do, but he doesn't love standing in a downpour to potty so sometimes he will urinate outside and then come inside and poop. It is obvious that he knows he has made a mistake because his facial expressions show me, but I have made a habit of not reacting strongly to his accidents. I always clean them up right away and simply tell him "no." Also important to remember is that Bichons sometimes take several minutes or even a walk to potty. Ricky and I are outside a lot and I am always surprised to see how many times he poops on a walk. But it's true, movement gets them "moving."

Rewarding Positive Behavior

"The key is to be consistent and use positive reinforcement. If you are giving treats as a reward, be sure to give them to them immediately after a successful elimination."

Betsy Savage
Dazzling Bichons

Rewarding positive behavior is an important training technique that will be key to potty training your puppy or dog. Bichons love to be rewarded and tend to respond poorly to negative reinforcement. It can be hard, but try not to yell at your puppy or adult dog, even when they do something bad; instead, encourage and reward good behavior. Bichons are stubborn and very sensitive and don't like to be yelled at. The best ideas are their ideas so if they don't like being yelled at they will likely just continue the behavior out of resentment. But they are also very food driven, so choose a healthy but tasty treat for them while they are training so they will be more motivated to be trained.

Photo Courtesy of Blanca Soto

A NOTE FROM RACHEL:

When my Bichon, Buddy, would be stubborn like that, we would joke that it was his royal lineage showing. Your puppy will love playing games and impressing you so make sure to work this into your potty training.

CHAPTER 7
Socializing with People and Animals

"Be sure not to expose your Bichon to other dogs until all their immunizations have taken effect. Once they have, you can let your puppy meet other dogs, but only dogs that are the same size or smaller at first and only dogs which you know are friendly and have their immunization as well."

Jeanette Neagu
Takoda Dogs

Photo Courtesy of Kim Cawley

Photo Courtesy of
Lorraine Cannon

The Importance of Good Socialization

Dogs are very social creatures and when they are not socialized properly, it can cause lasting behavioral issues. If your dog is never exposed to other people or animals other than those in your home, then he may be afraid of meeting new people or animals. This could cause your dog anxiety, fear, or even lead to aggression.

If your dog is properly socialized he will love meeting new dogs and people. Socialization is much easier to do with a puppy. If you have rescued an adult dog, there really is no way to tell how he has been socialized and he may be afraid or aggressive toward certain people. My dog Buddy was abused at a groomer, so he was terrified of going to a groomer or even having his nails trimmed or hair brushed by us. He also had an extreme fear of men. Luckily, through a lot of love and patience, he overcame some of those fears as he grew older.

If you have adopted an adult dog that was not socialized well as a puppy, this could be a challenging process, but know that with patience and practice your dog can feel comfortable around new people or animals. It is important to take small steps and ensure they are consistently comfortable in those steps before moving forward.

Additionally, all dogs and puppies have different personalities. Some might naturally be more shy. In that case, make sure you understand your new family member's personality. Socializing your dog does not mean he has to be outgoing, it just means he can comfortably meet new people or animals without feeling threatened.

Behavior Around Other Dogs

As a new dog or puppy parent you might be wary the first time you introduce your dog to other dogs. I know I was. When we first adopted our current dog and took her to the dog park for the first time, I kept her on a leash for quite a while before letting her off. What most people don't realize is most dogs can get defensive on a leash because they are restricted. So, how your dog meets other dogs on a leash is not necessarily how they will react in an open setting.

> **A NOTE FROM RACHEL:**
>
> *My dog Luna is not good at meeting dogs on a leash. If we meet a dog while on a walk, she is friendly with them but tends to get defensive quickly. When we go to the dog park, though, she is everybody's best friend. Being restricted by the leash is simply frustrating for her.*

While it is important to be cautious the first time you go to a dog park or when you first introduce dogs, at some point you also just have to take the leap. The first time you take your dog to the dog park, maybe go during a less busy time like a weekday afternoon or early weekend morning. The dog park is usually busiest right after work or on weekend afternoons.

Whether or not you are taking your dog to a dog park, on a walk, or maybe over to a friend or family member's house, you need to be aware of how your dog reacts and interacts with other dogs. Just like you don't like every single person you meet, your dog won't be best friends with every dog he or she meets.

Knowing this, you should know warning signs that mean your dog (or another dog) is agitated. The biggest signs are the hair rising on their back, growling, nipping, and yelping. Usually your dog will be tense and stand with muscles locked. If your dog is agitated, remove him from the situation to a safe place where he can calm down.

Bichons, as a breed, tend to be extremely friendly and non-aggressive. They love to play and socialize. While it is always important to be aware of your dog's reaction to other animals, they do pick up if you are tense or stressed. Try to stay calm and confident to put your dog at ease around other dogs.

Properly Greeting New People

Depending on the age and energy level of your new puppy or dog, he may or may not be inclined to meet new people. You probably have a sense of their general feelings toward new people from when the dog first met you. It is important to discourage your dog from jumping on other people as it can scare them, no matter how cute the dog is. Luckily, Bichons are small enough that if they jump on an adult they won't do much damage, but there is always the danger of them jumping on a small child. Even if it is just in excitement, which it likely is, it is always best to train your dog not to jump by telling them "off" and gently pushing him off of you and turning your body away from him while he is jumping. You can teach your family and guests to do this as well.

HELPFUL TIP
Proper Socialization

One mistake people make with small dogs like Bichons is being overprotective. This can lead to dogs who are fearful and even aggressive. Have the confidence to allow your Bichon puppy to socialize with people and dogs on its own so your Bichon can grow up being confident in its surroundings rather than leaning on you to protect it from the big, scary world.

If your dog is shy, start with one on one interactions with people you trust like a friend, parent, or sibling. Make sure that the people also know how to properly greet a dog. Usually, if a dog gets scared when meeting new people, it is because the people don't know how to greet a dog and not the other way around. Let them know not to pet or pick up your Bichon right away. Touch should be initiated by the dog and no one should pick him up until the dog has voluntarily climbed into their lap.

Smell is very important for dogs so the person greeting the dog should gently give the dog their hand to smell. If the dog is excited and positive then the person can go ahead and pet the dog. If he appears scared or intimidated, then the person should leave or step several feet back until your dog calms down. Be sure to give a lot of positive reinforcement. Once your dog is relaxed again, have the person come back. You could even give them a treat or toy to present to your dog. It is pretty amazing how convincing a bit of food can be for a dog!

If you have an outgoing dog, meeting new people might be no problem. For some dogs it is a breeze to meet new people, in fact, they love that there are new friends to show off their tricks to. In other cases, it might take a bit of time. This is completely unique to your dog and your situation. Similar to socializing your dog with other animals, you don't want to be too overprotective of your dog but you also don't want to cause them any extreme stress or agitation. It is okay to push your dog slightly outside his comfort zone, that is how dogs learn just like we do. Just be careful not to push too much too fast.

> **A NOTE FROM RACHEL:**
>
> *Some dogs are more comfortable with one gender over the other. My Bichon growing up did not like men. It was likely due to some trauma induced by a man when he was a puppy, but no one knows for sure. First, he got comfortable with my dad, then we introduced him to neighbors or other men. It is so important not to overwhelm your dog, especially if he is shy. Keep an eye on his demeanor and make sure he is comfortable.*

Bichon Frisés and Children

Bichons tend to love children because they are just playful kids themselves. They love to play and do tricks, but are always ready for some snuggle time or snacks. Dogs can have a very special connection with children and tend to take to them well.

> **A NOTE FROM RACHEL:**
>
> *My current dog, an 85-pound German Shepherd mix, was adopted a few years ago. While she has always been good with neighborhood children, she had never been around a newborn. A friend of ours had a baby and brought her over to visit. The parents laid the baby down in the middle of our floor. I was a bit nervous because Luna had never seen a baby before. I knew she wouldn't purposely harm the baby, but Luna is a large and powerful dog. Luna walked right up to the adorable baby, sniffed her head, gave her a kiss, and lay down right next to her. They were buddies the rest of the afternoon.*
>
> *My Bichon growing up was the same way, though in that case I was the kid. He was always playing outside with my sister and me and loved when our friends came over. We played soccer with him and attempted fetch, though he wasn't the most consistent at bringing the ball back! Some of my best memories growing up are with Buddy because he was just so great with my sister and me.*

Similar to the above section, it is important that the kids know how to approach a dog. One time, a small child ran up to Luna and jumped on her from behind. Luckily she didn't care, but not all dogs would react this way. Dogs don't like being surprised and approaching a dog from behind is never a good idea. No matter how kind the dog is, if he or she is startled they could nip or become agitated. All kids should approach all dogs slowly and let the dog sniff their hand. While they will likely become best friends this initial interaction is key to gaining trust between both the dog and the child. Make sure children meeting and playing with your dog know to be gentle.

Photo Courtesy of Laurie Crume

These steps are important to keep both the child and the dog safe. If you see the child becoming rough with your dog, kindly remind them the proper way to treat animals. Same goes for the dog. If your dog is becoming overexcited with the child, take your dog somewhere to relax and calm down. More often than not the overexcitement is simply that the kid and dog are having a lot of fun but there do need to be boundaries. All interactions between your dogs and small children should be supervised.

Ways to Socialize Your Dog with Other Pets

If you are bringing a puppy or dog into your home and already have another dog, you are going to want to make sure they are socialized with each other. It is important to know the personality of your existing pet to help with the socialization.

If you have a relaxed dog at home, then you may just be able to let the puppy loose. Just remember to have some focused one on one time with each of the dogs. They both need to feel loved both together and as individuals. In the next chapter we will specifically discuss how to introduce your new dog to other pets.

CHAPTER 8
Bichon Frise and Your Other Pets

"The first meeting between your new Bichon and current pets should be in a neutral spot, not in your home."

Karen Graeber
Whitebred Bichons

Introducing Your New Puppy to Other Animals

Cats

If you have cats as pets, bringing a puppy into the house could be a pretty hard sell. I have had cats my entire life; some love when you bring a new pet home, others are not so keen on the idea. Puppies are very curious and rambunctious and they will likely be very interested in their new sibling(s). Cats really don't like change so before the puppy even comes into the house you should start getting them acquainted with the puppy. If you have the chance to visit the puppy before you bring him home, rub a blanket or towel on him and then bring it home to the cats so they can get comfortable with his smell.

Photo Courtesy of Sherry Buckley

When you first bring the puppy home, be sure to keep the cats and the puppy separate. If your cats have a favorite spot or room in the house, keep them in there to start. You can also try using puppy gates to allow them to sniff each other. You will probably have to hold your cat gently on one side of the gate due to their ability to jump over.

Rub towels or blankets on the puppy and the cats to get their scent on them, then put the puppy's scented blanket with the cats and vice versa. This will get both the puppy and the cats acquainted with each other. If the cats are showing interest and the puppy isn't overwhelmed, it is okay to introduce them. Make sure to let the cats control the situation. If the puppy gets too excitable, then separate them and try again later.

HELPFUL TIP
Other Pets

As long as introductions are made properly, Bichons do well with other pets, including cats. Don't force interactions between your other pets and your new Bichon. With time, everybody should get along just fine.

It is also important to make sure the cats know they are still loved. Puppies are adorable and need a lot of attention, but don't neglect to give your cats love and attention or they may become jealous and act out against the puppy.

Dogs

Dogs tend to be pretty welcoming with puppies. It is still important to introduce them properly though. It completely depends on the personality of your current dog as to how to proceed. For many dogs, meeting a puppy is a fun and exciting experience. But some dogs are more possessive of their homes or their resources.

To introduce the puppy and the dog, take them both for walks and have them meet in neutral territory. If they are getting along well then walk them back to your house together. If at any point one of the dogs becomes agitated, separate them and try again later.

Be mindful that your current dog may have favorite toys, blankets, bones, or other resources that they may not want to share with the new puppy right away. Before bringing the puppy into the home, pick up your dog's favorite things, or anything that could cause jealousy or conflict.

Also, be aware that your current dog, or even your puppy, may not want to share your attention. Be careful not to make either dog feel left out, but especially your current dog, who probably feels a certain amount of "ownership" towards you.

Until you are certain that there are zero issues with aggression, do not leave them alone together. Once you are confident that your dog and puppy are good friends, you can leave them in the room together, but do not leave them home alone if you have any concerns for the safety of any of your animals. Also, be careful about feeding your pets together until you are certain that there aren't any issues with food guarding or aggression.

Introducing Your New Adult Dog to Other Animals

Cats

The process of introducing your new adult dog to cats and the process for introducing puppies and cats are very similar. The biggest difference is that your adult dog might already have an opinion of cats coming into the house whereas your puppy likely has never seen a cat before. Additionally, you are more likely to give the adult dog full access to the house more quickly than you would a puppy.

If your dog was fostered through a rescue, consult them based on if the dog interacted with cats at all and how the dog reacted. Most rescues will know if the dog is cat friendly or not, so be sure to check with them before adopting the dog.

When my husband and I were in the process of adopting an adult dog, we had two adult cats. Both were older; I had had them since I was a child. We knew that whatever dog we brought into our house had to be cat friendly. It was a requirement for us when we started looking for our new family member.

That being said, dogs and cats all have unique personalities and even if they are both okay with the other species, it might take a while for them to adjust to each other's presence. You should be sensitive to the dog's likely unknown past and also stay aware of your cat's stress level. You could keep your new dog leashed when they first meet the cat(s) so you have a bit more control over any reaction they might have.

> **A NOTE FROM RACHEL:**
>
> *It is completely possible and very normal for cats and dogs to coexist under the same roof. My dog, Luna, likes snuggling with one of our cats. However, knowing your pets' personalities is key. Our oldest cat, Tinkerbell, is a princess that does not like her nap time interrupted. Luna is a younger dog with quite a bit of energy. Their introduction wasn't necessarily the smoothest, but they have learned to respect each other's presence in the house and live in peace. Growing up, my Bichon, Buddy, loved our cats. He would chase them around the house and in the next moment they would be chasing him. They had a ton of fun together and played just like brothers and sisters.*

Dogs

Bringing an adult dog into a house with other adult dogs shouldn't be overly challenging, but might not be quite as simple as introducing your dog to a puppy. Once again, make sure the dogs meet on neutral territory. If your dog doesn't get possessive of the house or certain items in any way, then go ahead and bring the new dog in right away. Otherwise, put potential conflict causing items away and have an extra person there to help hold one pet while you focus your attention on the other pet.

While you will know your existing dog's personality, the same is not true for your new dog. Coming home can be very stressful. Be gentle and encouraging with both dogs as they meet and be sure to give both a lot of love. Your new dog might be very shy and your existing dog outgoing (or vice versa). If the new dog is agitated or very shy when you are bringing him or her home, remove the other dog from the room or the house so the new dog can calm down before meeting the other members of his or her new family. Then, once the dog is calm, take him to meet his new brother or sister on neutral territory.

Once again, provide supervision while your pets get to know each other and if one pet is much larger or more aggressive, keep them in separate locations for their safety and comfort.

> **A NOTE FROM KRIS:**
>
> *When I brought Ricky home, he immediately decided that I belonged to him. When my older dog Zuki tried to come to get attention from me, he snapped at her. He has only done this three times in about as many years, but simply and firmly telling him no has been enough to keep this behavior at bay.*

Pack Mentality

"Fortunately the Bichon adapts very well in almost any household. I always tell my customers that the pet that is there first gets to pull rank. Once that is established the Bichon will be their best friend."

Vicki Turner
Turner Dog Ranch

Though dogs have been domesticated for tens of thousands of years, they still have some of their initial instincts left in their blood. One of these instincts is pack mentality. If you have a multi-dog household you might see some of this. Even if you just have one dog, he is likely looking to you as his alpha to guide him and keep him in line.

If you have a multi-dog household you might see some signs of dominance between the dogs. It is usually pretty easy to notice if a dog is dominant or submissive. If one of your dogs lies down on their back for another dog, that is submissive behavior.

You need to make sure you are the alpha in the household by providing structure and safety for all of the pets in your home. If your dog deems itself an alpha, then he will have control of the house, at least in his eyes. In order to be the alpha, you need to earn the respect of your dog. This does not mean yelling at them or showing any other type of force, but merely being a constant presence for your dog. You can show dominant behavior in simple actions such as feeding your dog at the same time every day or going through doors first. Another great way to assert dominance is to take your dog on a walk on the leash, occasionally offering commands like sit, stay, or shake. Also, don't let your dog show signs of dominance like taking your spot on the couch or bed. If you earn the respect of your dog, then he will respect and love you on a whole new level.

Fighting and Bad Behavior

If your dog is getting into trouble, it often points to two main possibilities: improper training or boredom. It is possible your dog could have some inherent behavioral issues but improper training and boredom are good places to start for evaluation purposes.

If you have allowed your dog to be alpha, then they might fight or exhibit bad behavior in order to remain the alpha. You will have to retake your alpha spot to keep their respect and behavior in line. Do not send your dog mixed signals about their behavior. Make sure that you are praising good behavior and decreasing negative behavior by ignoring it or correcting it. If you have not taken your dog to obedience training, or if your at-home training has been thus far ineffective, it would be a good idea to check out training classes in your area. While obedience training is meant to teach your dog basic commands, it is also a time of bonding for both you and your dog, and is a useful reminder to your dog that you are in charge in a respectful and loving way.

If your dog does not have a good outlet for their energy such as exercise, walks or playtime, they could turn to destructive or aggressive behavior to release the energy they have. This can happen if they are crated or alone during the day and don't get adequate exercise when you get home. Dog parks are a great asset as a dog owner which not only will physically tire your dog out but also mentally engage them. While walks and runs are great for dogs, they also need to exercise their brains. This could be done with socialization with other dogs, or even puzzles or games.

Raising Multiple Puppies from the Same Litter

It is important to say this upfront: it is highly discouraged to raise two puppies from the same litter. The fact of the matter is, they don't usually bond better if they are from the same litter and more likely than not you will not be able to give both puppies the time they need. If your rationale is that they will keep each other busy, then that should be a huge red flag. If you don't have time to care for one puppy, getting two to keep each other company is not the answer.

That being said, if you do decide to raise multiple puppies from the same litter there are a few things to be aware of. First, be sure to give them separate crates. As discussed earlier, crates can become a safe haven or bedroom for your dog. Giving them each their own space is generally a

Photo Courtesy of Nancy Byrne

good idea. Additionally, they will be spending the majority of their time together so some alone time could be beneficial for keeping them interested in playing with each other, and allowing them to have time to enjoy their favorite toys or bones without competition or sharing. Additionally, giving them alone time will help build their confidence in being alone.

You should also train them separately. This could be a chore but it is the reality of bringing two new puppies into your house. Training your dog should be a one on one bonding experience. Each dog will respond differently to training and you will want to have a unique bond with each dog. However, it can be beneficial to train them around adult dogs because adult dogs often set the example of the behavior you are hoping to see out of your puppies.

> **A NOTE FROM KRIS:**
>
> *My dog Zuki has always been great at "training" younger dogs. For example, she has taught two puppies to sit by using her paw to push their bottoms down so that she and the puppy can both earn a treat for "sitting." Training dogs around Zuki has always been pretty easy because she helps enforce positive behaviors.*

Make sure that each puppy also gets general one on one time whether it be on walks, playing, or general socializing. They need to develop as individuals and learn to socialize separately so that neither becomes dependent on the other one for confidence. If one of the dogs becomes dependent on the other, then the shyer dog is more likely to be afraid whenever it is separated from its brother or sister. Also, this can be an issue if you try to allow them to play with other dogs together because if they become territorial of one another, then they might not welcome other dogs into their play circle; this can even lead to aggression. Also, they may not want to play or walk without their sibling if they do not experience regular time away from their sibling. Make sure that you teach them how to get along and play nicely, but also how to be well adjusted and confident on their own.

Options if Your Pets Don't Get Along

When you bring a new pet into the family, it might not go as smoothly as hoped. It could take a while for them to get along well. You shouldn't be concerned if there is some tension; this is normal. But it is important to do everything you can to ease the tension, thus creating a safe environment for them both,

The biggest action you can take is to make sure each animal knows they are loved and gets adequate time and attention. Playing, walks, and snuggling are all great activities to do with your pets. Give your pet time alone with you. Give them the gift of undivided attention to help them feel a strong bond that give them the assurance they need to trust the world enough to want to be a vibrant and healthy part of it.

If you have two dogs that don't get along, you can encourage bonding by taking them on walks together. You can also tire each of them out separately and then work on introducing them. Tiring dogs out is a great way to encourage good behavior. It is also a great way to remind them that you appreciate them as individuals, or as a pair.

Make sure you establish yourself as the alpha in the household and that you execute this position mindfully. If you are gentle but unwavering in your expectations, this can encourage the dogs to get along. Remember to be patient and don't give up on helping them building a positive relationship.

CHAPTER 9
Physical and Mental Exercise

"They don't need much exercise, but are very capable on going on short runs with their owners. Simply walking and running around in the yard often is enough. Nothing is more fun than to watch a Bichon 'blitz' when they are happy."

Vicki Turner
Turner Dog Ranch

Photo Courtesy of
Sue Bailey

Exercise Requirements

While your Bichon probably won't run five miles with you, the breed does love to play and is considered to have moderate energy levels. They do not do well cooped up all day. Bichons do not need rigorous exercise, but they love playtime and walks.

Bichons are very social dogs who love to do tricks so using the time to train and challenge their brains is always fun for everyone involved. Playtime could be around the house, in the yard, or at the dog park.

Sometimes your Bichon will get what is referred to as the "Bichon Buzz," which is a seemingly instant burst of energy. Growing up, Buddy would be sleeping next to me on the couch and all of a sudden, he would get up and do a bunch of laps around the coffee table at full speed before settling down on the couch again. It was adorable and funny.

Some of my best memories as a kid are playing outside with Buddy. When we were really little he would jog alongside my sister and me on our bikes around the block or jump around as we played in the backyard. He was perfect for our energy level.

Bichons are people and family dogs who have enough energy for fun playtime but also appreciate some good old-fashioned snuggling at the end of the day.

Different Types of Exercise to Try

Bichons aren't really picky about their type of exercise, but they do require some form of physical and mental stimulation every day. They are not the type of dog who is content with one or two long walks a week; instead, your Bichon will likely prefer shorter bursts of exercise every day of the week.

Photo Courtesy of
Melissa Platt

Walks

Walks are a great way to physically and mentally stimulate your dog. A 30-minute walk should be good, though your dog might prefer one that's longer. Walking on pavement is also good to keep your dog's nails healthy and filed down.

If you have kids, you can send them for a walk after school or dinner. Otherwise, an evening walk with your dog is fun. It promotes a healthy relationship and helps foster a strong bond. You can also work on training during your walk, which will further mentally stimulate your dog. Bichons are motivated by exploring, treats, and human companionship, making walks and walk training a wonderful experience for your Bichon.

Dog Park

The dog park is one of the best ways to physically and mentally tire your dog out. It's great for socialization. A lot of dog parks will have a small dog area that's perfect for your little Bichon to buzz around in. Some Bichons can definitely hang with the bigger dogs as well.

The dog park was instrumental in socializing my current dog. She was abused in her first home and once she was settled into our home, we started taking her to the dog park. I was nervous at first, but she had been friendly with all of the dogs in our neighborhood. Initially, I just wanted to keep her on the leash but that is actually a big mistake as dogs can get defensive on a leash.

Another lesson I learned was not to take treats into the dog park. Dogs can sniff out treats from a mile away and if you give your dog a treat then all of them will want treats. If you do want to give a dog a treat, make sure you ask the dog's owner prior to doling out the food.

Toys

From chew toys to balls to squeaky toys, dogs love their toys. Toys like balls or ropes are great for you to play with your dog but can also be entertaining when your dog is alone. You will find that your dog will probably prefer a certain type of toy or have a favorite toy.

Photo Courtesy of
Colleen & Oliver Peterson

Buddy loved this zebra squeaky toy that he carried around and wore out constantly. We always had extra zebra squeaky toys lying around for when his current one would get lost or ruined. Without fail every time we moved the couch, we found a lost zebra or other dog toys underneath it.

There are also puzzle games you can buy which are great for Bichons as they are usually quite smart and love a challenge. More so than the challenge itself, they love to show off their skills and impress their family. Beware though, once they figure it out, they might want to keep doing it to keep getting a positive reaction out of you!

Importance of Mental Exercise

In most respects, mental exercise is just as important as physical exercise and can be just as exhausting. You need to find a balance between the two. Letting your dog out in the yard might be good physical exercise but probably doesn't encourage much mental stimulation.

When your dog doesn't get mental exercise it can get mischievous, which tends to get them into trouble. Bichons aren't notorious for having behavioral problems; however, any bored dog will need an outlet for his energy.

Mental exercise can be as simple as teaching your Bichon to play fetch or Frisbee. This is both physically and mentally stimulating, making it a great activity for Bichons. You can also hide a few treats in your house or in the yard and teach your Bichon to search for them. Bubbles are also fun for many dogs and are very inexpensive. Try tug of war with a small knotted rope, or purchase food puzzle games to challenge your pup to find the food in the hidden compartments. If you are feeling ambitious, work on setting up a small (or elaborate) obstacle course for your Bichon. Consider adding a bench to climb on, a seesaw, a tube to crawl through, or low poles to jump over (simply called "jumps").

Most importantly, try to think of playing with your Bichon as a time for joy and bonding rather than as an obligation. Bichons are great lapdogs and will love you no matter what you are doing with them, but they will have so much fun trying new games, and you will too when you see how much fun they are having.

Photo Courtesy of
Pam Volkert

CHAPTER 10
Training Your Bichon Frise

Setting Clear Expectations

Setting clear expectations is key to successfully training your dog, especially a Bichon Frise who truly just wants to please you. If you set clear expectations for both you and your dog and are consistent with the training, he will respond well to the training you provide.

It is important that anyone else handling the dog on a regular basis, such as family members, is aware of the expectations you are setting. Without clear expectations, your dog may be harder to train because he's confused.

Photo Courtesy of
Michelle Womack

Operant Conditioning Basics

Operant conditioning is a form of training and behavior modification that developed from B.F. Skinner's 1930s research that hypothesized that behaviors that are reinforced are more likely to be repeated. These consequences, reinforcements, rewards, or punishments are referred to as "operants." Without knowing, we are reinforcing behaviors all of the time. Without meaning to, we may even be encouraging the very behaviors we wish to diminish. This section will focus on how we can behave in a way that encourages (reinforces) the behavior we wish to see in our dogs (like sitting and going potty outdoors) and decreases the behaviors we don't like (such as play biting or pulling on the leash.) In short, we will discuss how our responses affect, and even determine, our dog's behavior.

For example, operant conditioning can be used to train your dog to walk next to you and not pull on the leash. When he does a good job and walks next to you without pulling, you give him a treat or simply say, "What a good boy!" When he pulls on the leash, you verbally correct him or stop walking until he calms himself. If your dog wants to continue walking, then he will learn not to pull on the leash to receive treats and to continue walking. If he pulls, you stop. If he stops pulling, leaving slack in the leash, you praise and offer a treat, then continue walking. Your response, in time, will determine his behavior. Conversely, if you keep walking, allowing your dog to drag you during the walk, you are effectively saying, "I am okay with this, and we will keep walking no matter how you behave." You would then be setting the stage for walks that you might truly dread, and you may eventually decide that walking your dog is just too hard, which may lead to other undesirable behavior in your Bichon because he has not received enough exercise or opportunities to relieve himself outdoors.

In order for you to decide how you should respond to your dog's various behaviors, we must distinguish the difference between the types of possible responses and the likely effects they will have on your Bichon. The different forms are as follows: positive reinforcement, negative punishment, negative reinforcement, and positive punishment. I have listed these forms of operant conditioning from the most effective and cruelty free, to the least effective and potentially most fear inducing. Additionally, it's important to define positive and negative, as well as reinforcement and punishment, as these terms are used differently than we use them typically and without defining them, there could be considerable confusion moving forward.

Defining Positive and Negative

When it comes to operant conditioning, "positive" simply means that you are giving something such as a treat or a toy. "Negative" means to take something away. You could take away a toy or even attention. You can even "take away" something annoying, like the beeping of an electronic collar. Negative does not necessarily mean bad or harmful, and positive does not have to mean good or enjoyable. Think of positive or negative like you do in math; it is either adding or subtracting a factor.

Defining Reinforcement and Punishment

Reinforcement is a term used to define behavior on our part that encourages the repeated behavior on the part of our dog. Punishment is a term used to define our behavior toward the dog that is used to decrease the likelihood of a certain dog behavior continuing.

Positive Reinforcement

Positive reinforcement is considered the most beneficial way to train a dog when using Operant Conditioning. It is also the easiest for most people to understand and implement. I will offer two inverse examples of when positive reinforcement is likely to increase desirable behaviors in your dog, and when it could increase undesirable behaviors.

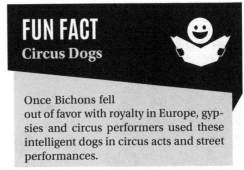

FUN FACT
Circus Dogs

Once Bichons fell out of favor with royalty in Europe, gypsies and circus performers used these intelligent dogs in circus acts and street performances.

Example A: To increase the likelihood that your Bichon will sit on command, you can give him a treat when he sits (even if imperfectly). He will associate the reward and the command and will learn that he must sit to get a treat.

Example B: Your Bichon stares at you while you eat and begs for food. If you give him food from your plate, you will likely increase the frequency of his begging behavior. IGNORE HIM!

In both of these examples, you are giving your Bichon reinforcement and encouraging the behaviors. Be sure to only use positive reinforcement with the behaviors you want to see continue. Positive reinforcement can be a very beneficial training technique, especially for Bichons who want to impress you and make you happy.

If you use positive reinforcement correctly you will likely get great results while training your dog. For example, if your dog comes on command and you give him a treat, he will likely continue to come on command. You can give attention, food, treats, or toys, to name a few. Most Bichons are going to be motivated simply from your loving attention.

Negative Punishment

Negative punishment is taking something away to stop or decrease an action in your dog. This is used quite often for training dogs. For example, if your dog barks a lot you can stop giving him attention, basically ignoring him, and he will likely bark less because he likes attention from you. Punishment need not be harsh or cruel. Negative punishment is simply taking away something that your dog desires to get him to stop doing something that you don't desire to see continue.

This can work against you, though, if you aren't careful. For example, my dog knows when I put on my shoes I am leaving, so she refuses to come

*Photo Courtesy of
Colleen & Oliver Peterson*

inside. She doesn't want me to leave and knows the action of coming into the house will trigger me leaving the house. Or, if you take your dog to the dog park and the only time you call them to you is when you are ready to leave, they will associate leaving with your call meaning they are less likely to come to you willingly because they want to stay at the park.

Another example of an appropriate negative punishment would be picking up your dog's water if he is splashing in it and giving it back to him (positive reinforcement) when he is sitting calmly. However, you would be using this technique improperly if you were to deprive your dog of water for a period of time because he is a messy drinker or likes to stand in his water. Moreover, your dog wouldn't likely understand the correlation between his splashing and you taking away his water for a few hours. He would simply be thirsty and may continue to play in his water when you finally give it back to him, causing him to drink too fast and get sick. And now there's a whole new mess to clean.

Negative Reinforcement

Negative reinforcement is taking something away or stopping something when the dog does a certain action to increase the frequency of their behavior. Similar to positive punishment, negative reinforcement is not usually recommended. So in most cases, something bad is happening to the dog and they stop the action to make the unpleasant action stop.

One of the most common forms of negative reinforcement is a choke collar or a pronged collar to prevent a dog from pulling during a walk. The dog will probably stop pulling in order to make the discomfort go away. This is different from positive punishment in that the dog is doing an action to stop the discomfort of the choke collar as opposed to receiving a shock for doing an action that the trainer deems undesirable.

Another example of negative reinforcement is a bark collar that does not shock the dog, but only beeps at them when they bark. The idea is that the dog will stop barking to stop hearing the annoying beep when they bark.

Going back to operant conditioning definitions, remember that negative reinforcement is taking something away when an action is done. Usually with dogs, it is relieving some form of pain when the correct action is done, such as a shock collar or choke collar. So, you will stop pulling on the choke collar or applying the shock collar when they do the correct action.

When negative reinforcement is used it is more of reacting to bad behavior as opposed to encouraging good behavior. When you react to bad

behavior it might not be consistent enough for the dog to understand what they are getting punished for.

Using negative reinforcement that includes some form of pain can cause your dog to be scared or even resent you. You have to be sure to find the balance between earning respect and scaring your dog. Choose your reinforcements carefully and kindly.

Positive Punishment

In the case of your dog jumping on you, a "positive punishment" would be to slap him on the nose or to shove him with your foot. You are giving a slap or shove in response to him jumping on you. You can see how positive punishment is not an appropriate training technique. It builds fear and hostility in a dog, rather than increasing the bond between you.

Instead of using this form of conditioning, you could tell your Bichon to sit, and give him attention and praise when he does. Now you are increasing the desired behavior while also putting the safety of your dog first.

Shock collars are a very common form of positive punishment usually used to prevent a dog from barking, jumping, or being destructive. Oftentimes people without training knowledge will use a shock collar or other forms of positive punishment because they lack the experience or expertise to know how to offer a positive reinforcement. However, some people understand how to use a positive reinforcement, but choose not to do so because they feel that it would take longer to achieve their training goals. And to some degree this might be true. However, hurting a dog to get them to obey you will create fear and confusion. It is better to give your Bichon opportunities to be rewarded than to take shortcuts that hurt your dog and your relationship with him.

You may have already used operant conditioning on previous animals or even your kids. In fact, it probably happened to you when you are growing up or even still as an adult. For example, if your kid won't eat their dinner and you take away dessert, that is negative reinforcement. Taking away dessert will encourage your kid to eat their dinner.

This is not just a technique, it is simply a way that as living beings we respond to actions and things around us. Dogs are the same way. Having a basic understanding of operant conditioning is a good start to training your dog.

Primary Reinforcements

We are going to focus on positive reinforcement, as it is usually the most effective way to train your dog. Bichons, in particular, respond well to positive reinforcement. They love to impress you so positive reinforcement will make them want to do actions more.

There are three primary reinforcements you will want to have in your court when you are training your puppy or dog: food, toys, and play time. These are rewards that your dog will likely value enough so they will listen to you. Dogs are very smart and enjoy getting rewards for the work they do.

It is important to have "high-value" food treats. When we were going through obedience training with my dog, we had generic treats. We could not get her to focus or listen even though she was an adult and had been very focused in the past. The trainer saw us struggling and walked over. She simply handed us a cut up hot dog. After Luna tasted the hot dog and realized that was her reward for listening, she learned her commands very quickly. For Luna, the hot dog was a treat worth working for, but our original treats were not.

Using a valuable toy as a reward can significantly increase your training results. If your dog is not showing interest in the toy you are using, it might just be that they don't feel the reward you are trying to give them is worth the effort. Try different toys to see what your Bichon likes, and when you find the right one, buy a few! When your dog is doing something you like, for example sitting calmly and quietly in the car, you can give him the toy as a special reward.

When you get home from work, your Bichon may be ready to play, but you might need a minute to change clothes and unwind a bit. If you are not ready to play, it's important not to send mixed signals. Tend to the things you need to tend to first and if your dog is ready to play when you are, but not jumping on you or biting you to get your attention, grab the tennis ball and enjoy some playtime with your buddy!

It is important only to use primary reinforcements when they do something good or are behaving in a way that you want them to. If you give your dog a treat or toy after they exhibit bad behavior, it can encourage said behavior.

Secondary Reinforcements

Secondary reinforcements are also a great tool to use. You won't always have treats on you, and don't want your dog to get in the habit of only listening for a reward. Once they are trained, they should identify the word or signal you use for a command and do it without needing a primary reinforcement as a reward.

While primary reinforcements are awesome for training your dog, and should be incorporated throughout their life, they will likely be the most heavily used when you are first training your puppy or dog. As they learn the command itself, you should slowly reduce the amount of times you give them the primary reward and work in a secondary reward. A secondary reward is still something good that they can earn, but is not as satisfying as food, toys, or playtime. Common forms of secondary reinforcement are attention, praise, and a clicker.

Attention can come in the form of simply sitting with your Bichon. In the evening, my Bichon knows that we are about to spend time together when I get a throw blanket and head to the couch. He gets so excited! Then he calmly lies in my lap and I pet him while we watch TV. Attention may not be a tangible reward, but it is certainly one that dogs live for.

Praise is a great way to reward your dog for listening. Bichons love praise and will do nearly anything to get it. As you proceed in your training, giving your dog attention and praise for doing good actions can start to replace primary reinforcements. Often when I praise my Bichon, or tell him how much I love him, he tilts his head and watches me intently like he is trying to soak it all in. As a dog care provider, I have seen the power of praise in many dogs, and I haven't met a dog who doesn't love a good word. When paired with a soothing or appropriately direct tone of voice, the desired results in training will be achieved even more quickly.

The same goes for using a clicker. This is a very common secondary reinforcement that is used. When you first start using a clicker do it in conjunction with a primary reinforcement (usually a treat) so the dog identifies the click with a positive action. Clickers are small, nondescript, and are used for positive reinforcement as opposed to some other training techniques such as a shock collar which can hurt or scare your dog. A lot of obedience training schools will introduce a clicker. In order for the clicker to be effective, it needs to be used consistently and trained correctly.

Hiring a Trainer and Attending Classes

Training is important for both you and your dog. Even if you have trained a dog in the past or done obedience training classes before, the classes can be a good way to socialize with your puppy and is a set-aside amount of time that you will have with your dog every week.

There are likely several places in your area that offer basic obedience training classes. Some of the most common include pet stores, doggy day cares, and groomers. There are even businesses whose sole focus is to train dogs. Sometimes local shelters or humane societies will also offer reasonably priced obedience training.

Another form of training is to hire a trainer. There are companies and individuals who will come to your house and give obedience classes. It is a great way to get one on one training with your dog. Many times, this kind of training is used for off-leash training or other higher-level commands; however, it can be a great option for basic obedience training if you or your dog might not benefit in a big group setting.

Owner Behavior

As an owner, your behavior is key to the success of your dog's training. Dogs, like many animals, feed off the emotions and reactions of those they love. If you are sick or having a bad day, you might find your dog being a little extra snuggly. If you are aggressive toward other dogs or people, your dog will pick up on that as well.

If you stay calm in situations it can help keep your dog calm as well. You are an example for your dog, though no matter how calm you are, he might still be afraid of the vacuum! Your reaction in public and private can act as guide for your dog, even though he might not always react the same way.

CHAPTER 11
Basic Commands

Benefits of Proper Training

HELPFUL TIP
Training Tips

Bichons are easier to train than many other small breeds of dog thanks to their combination of intelligence and desire to please people. Take advantage of this combination by using positive reinforcement regularly to emphasize the behaviors you want your Bichon to display.

Properly training your dog has benefits that could last their lifetime. Investing in training, whether it is a class or a personal trainer, is important for both you and your dog and could even save his life someday. At some point during your dog's life he will probably run away or get off his leash. For some dog owners this is a fairly regular occurrence if their dogs are adventurous or skittish. There are so many ways your dog could get out of his collar, sneak out the door, or accidentally get away. If your dog is trained to stop when you call a certain command or knows to come back when you call his name, this could save his life by preventing him from running into a busy street or getting permanently lost.

Additionally, training provides a great jumping off point for your relationship with your dog and the mutual respect you have for each other. Even if your dog has only mastered a few basic commands like sit and come, that's a solid base that can make future training easier. Also, it gives your dog the understanding that you are the boss and sets clear expectations.

Your Bichon will probably take his training very seriously and work hard to impress you. The great thing about training is it does not ever have to end. There are multiple levels of training from basic to advanced, agility training, off leash training, and so many more in between.

Bichons particularly thrive in a training environment where they can show off. There is nothing your Bichon will love more than spending time with you and learning new commands. Keep this in mind as you work your way through the basic commands and develop a strong bond with your dog.

Picking the Right Rewards or Treats

When I first got my dog a few years ago, I thought a treat was a treat. I was so incredibly wrong. Treats are not all created equal and what one dog values as the greatest treat in the world another might stick his nose up at and refuse to eat.

If you don't offer your dog something of value in return for their effort and hard work of learning commands, they likely won't listen. Not all dogs are food motivated though. Those that aren't tend to be motivated by toys or play time. Some even love walks as a reward. When you first bring home your dog, there will likely be some trial and error to find the perfect fit for a reward. I can personally attest to that struggle which can be supported by the shelf in my pantry dedicated to dog treats we tried before cricket treats did the trick.

If you have a dog that loves a specific type of toy, such as a plush toy with a squeaker or a ball, that in itself can be a reward. If you use a toy, make sure to designate a specific toy for training time. If the dog has access to the toy all of the time, it won't become as exciting or rewarding.

Photo Courtesy of
Cindy Cho

Different Training Methods

There is a plethora of different training methods out there and all have their benefits. There will always be new training methods that come out, but the core training methods have been used for a long time and have had proven success.

Positive reinforcement was discussed in chapter 10 and is one of the most common types of training. Positive reinforcement is giving the dog a reward or treat immediately after he performs a desired action.

Clicker training can be used in conjunction with a treat and verbal cue to signal your dog has done a good job. Eventually, your Bichon will learn to use the clicker as the reward, though treats will still be appreciated! The clicker can come in handy if you travel or go to a dog park a lot and can't always have treats on you.

Mirror training is a fun way to train your dog. Dogs are pack animals and learn from each other. If you have a friend or family member with a well-behaved dog that gets along with your pet, you can use this method to develop good behaviors. My own dog learned how to run next to me using this method. Before I trained her to run next to me, she would zigzag and trip me up. After a few runs and walks with a friend whose dog was well behaved on runs, my dog started to "mirror" that behavior and, while there are still some times where we struggle, it is much better.

One of the most popular types of training is relationship-based training. This is a very personalized approach which is based on the relationship you have with your dog. It is not a one size fits all training solution but is catered to both you and your dog's personalities and the bond you are hoping to form. It usually combines some of the types of training listed above.

Many people use a combination of training methods that best fit their lifestyles and goals of training. You may just want your dog to behave and know basic commands but someone else reading this book might want a dog that can be trained off leash or even enter agility competitions.

Basic Commands

The key to teaching your dog basic commands is to be consistent and be aware of his attention span. Puppies have significantly lower attention spans than adult dogs, though both will need breaks. Make sure you pick a spot in your house that does not have a lot of distractions to work with your dog on commands. Try to stop people from coming in and out of the area or causing distractions while you are training your dog.

If you're using treats, make sure you break them up into smaller pieces so you don't make your dog sick or overdo the calories.

Sit

First, it's important to get your dog's attention. This can simply be done by standing in front of your dog and saying his name. Make sure your dog knows you have the treat in your hand. You can even show him the treat.

Start with the treat very close to your dog's nose, then slowly move it over the top of his head. He will likely try to follow it and the movement will naturally move him into the sitting position. As he sits down, give the verbal command, "Sit." As soon as he performs the command, give him the treat and a lot of praise.

Work on this motion with the treat until your dog has gotten it down. If he is struggling to understand, you can very gently guide his bottom into the sitting position. Be very careful, though, as pushing too hard could hurt your dog. Keep the treat close to his head so there is very little room for him to twist or jump to try and get the treat.

If you have a high-energy dog that is having trouble focusing, you can try taking him for a walk or having play time before working on his training. Additionally, you can use a leash to keep him a bit more under control in the room.

Practice makes perfect when it comes to training so spend time every day working on the commands with your dog. If he doesn't get it right away, it's okay. Different dogs will work at different paces. Try not to get frustrated at your dog. Bichons specifically hate to disappoint their owners so be sure to encourage effort and work with your dog through any frustration.

Stay

After learning the sit command, stay is a natural progression. Stay will have two commands. The first is to initiate the command with which you will probably say "stay." The second will be to release your dog from the command. I personally use "okay" but "all done" and "release" are also very common release words for dogs. Whatever it is, make sure you are consistent with what you say.

Refrain from using terms such as "good dog" or "good girl" as releases because you will likely use that when talking to your dog in other ways other than when working on a command.

Learning the stay command can take time and patience because your dog is probably going to want to be next to you. Start out by having him sit down. Then take one step away while saying "stay." If he does that successfully, say the release in a voice that gets him excited to come to you and reward with a treat.

Slowly start moving further away and having him hold the command for longer periods of time. Make sure you take your time and don't work on duration and distance at the same time. Work on one, then the other, then mix up your distance from your dog and the duration of the command.orking on a command.

This is a tough command especially for puppies to learn because they usually don't have the attention span to sit still for periods of time. After your dog has mastered stay in a distraction free environment, you can work to introduce distractions such as someone walking through the room, taking him outside, or placing the treat in front of him so he can see it and having him wait for the release before he gets it.

Lie Down

If your dog has learned to sit and stay, then lie down should be fairly easy. Have your dog sit down, then give a reward. Don't release your dog from the sit command. Have a second treat handy. While saying "down" or "lie down," slowly move the treat forward from your dog's nose.

As you move the treat forward along the ground, the dog's natural reaction should be to lie down. If you go too quickly your dog will probably just stand up and walk to get the treat. To help with the movement, you can put your hand on your dog's shoulder and gently guide him into the down position.

This is a very natural position for dogs, so training them to lay down on command is usually one of the easier basic commands to teach.

Come

This is one of the most important skills, and the one that is most likely to save your dog's life. If your dog is running for a busy road or by a car, having a good recall could literally be the difference between life and death. There are several steps to training a good recall. Some will require a second person so if you have a friend, significant other, or sibling, enlist their help.

The easiest way to start is to make it a game. Some call it back and forth or tug of war. Stand across from your friend or family member. Maybe start around ten feet away. Each of you should have a toy or treats in your hand

Photo Courtesy of
Tammy Capozzoli

or pocket. One person should show the treat or toy and say the dog's name and "come." Act very excited like it is a game. Then when the dog comes to you give him a treat and a lot of praise. Before the dog can get distracted, the other person will do the same thing.

As the dog understands the game, start spreading out further or let the dog start running and call him back. By making it a game the dog thinks it is fun.

Stay consistent with your command so as not to confuse your dog. Additionally, don't only call your dog when you are going to do something he doesn't necessarily like such as giving him a bath or clipping his nails. This is especially true when you're first training. You don't want any negative experiences when he is first learning the command.

After your dog masters the tug of war game and the "come" command, increase the level of difficulty; you can take your dog out in the yard. As he gets better at following the command you can slowly increase the number of distractions.

Off/Down

Dogs love to jump. They want to be close to your face. And while you might think it's adorable, many people don't agree.

There are two main ways to train your dog to stay off: a command and a lack of action.

When your dog jumps on you, say "off" or "down." Whichever command you choose, stay consistent. When all four of your dog's paws are firmly on the ground, give the treat and a lot of praise. You can even show him the treat before you give the command to get his focus.

It's important not to yell at your dog. If your dog is not responding well to a verbal command, you can choose a literal lack of action instead to teach him not to jump.

When your dog jumps, turn around and show him your back. Don't engage with your dog at all until he calms down, then give him some attention. If you make the jumping a non-event and ignore your dog completely, he will associate not getting attention with jumping and learn to stop.

Give/Drop

Whether your dog loves to pick up and chew on random things, so it's a safety issue, or you simply want him to drop a toy when you're playing fetch, this is a great command for all dogs to learn.

Most dogs learn well when you start with the trade method. If your dog has a toy or object you want him to give up, offer a piece of a treat, say "give" or "drop," and trade with your dog. If he won't trade with you, you can try a higher value treat.

Be careful not to force the toy out of your dog's mouth. You want him to think the trade is a good thing, not a bad one. Use consistent commands every time you offer them the trade.

It's best to say the command, then offer the treat. Breaking the training for this command up into small, consistent doses, such as five minutes three times a day, will avoid overwhelming or overfeeding your dog.

This can be a tough command to master, especially if a dog really loves a toy you want him to give up.

Walk

Taking your dog for short and long walks can help him learn to be comfortable on the leash and even enjoy it. Every time I open the closet to get my shoes, my dog goes nuts because she thinks she gets "to go with." One of my friend's dogs loves walks so much he will go and get his leash anytime he wants to go out, which is quite often!

Walking is a necessary skill for a healthy dog; and the better your dog is on the leash, the more likely you are to want to walk him. Also teaching him to walk properly and calmly will help prevent injury to your dog from being disorderly and even jerking his body and head in a way that hurts his neck. Whether you feel that your dog needs leash training or not, consider the reality that he will need to be on a leash at some point, whether going to the vet, to the airport, to the dog park, or even to a cookout. Consistent leash training can help set you and your Bichon up for a lifetime of enjoyment walking together and just moving about town as a team.

It's important to introduce your dog to the collar, harness, or leash quite early once you bring him home. You can start in the house. Some puppies will try to get out of their collar but offering treats and rewards for good behavior goes a long way. It may seem weird to walk around your house with your dog on his leash but it's good for him to get used to it with minimal distractions.

If your dog pulls, you can use the tree method to discourage it. Basically the tree method is: if your dog pulls, simply stand there and don't interact with your dog or let him go anywhere until he stops. Once your dog settles down, reward with a treat, then keep walking.

When you're first training your dog, no matter the age, this can be a very frustrating and slow process. When we were first leash training my dog Luna, it could take 20 minutes just to get down the block and back. As long as you are patient, it will eventually pay off.

If your dog gets excited and chases something, promptly turn around and start walking the other way. This will break your dog's focus and he will be forced to walk the direction you are going. It isn't always possible to do this, and in such cases try to distract your dog with a treat to get his focus back on you and the walk.

Advanced Commands

There are so many commands you can learn with your dog. If you have a dog that loves to do tricks or learn new things, which is very possible for a Bichon, then having a lot of them in your arsenal is a great way to bond with your dog and keep him mentally engaged.

Some advanced commands could include paw, spin, crawl, roll over, leave it, and so many more. There are some great tools out there for learning and teaching advanced commands.

There are also advanced obedience training classes and agility classes that are great options if you love bonding with your dog through training.

CHAPTER 12
Dealing with Unwanted Behaviors

"My Bichon has the bad habit of barking at people until she gets to sniff them. She also barks at animals on TV. Sometimes I just have to shut it off and stay away from Animal Planet!"

Betsy Savage
Dazzling Bichons

Photo Courtesy of
Cindy Gelnette

What Is Bad Behavior in Dogs?

There are so many things that could be considered bad behavior in dogs, but ultimately, bad behavior can be whittled down to when your dog doesn't meet your expectations. This could be small actions like jumping on the couch or bed, if that is an expectation you hold, or larger misdeeds such as exhibiting aggression.

HELPFUL TIP
Bichons Like Company

Since Bichons were bred to be companion dogs, they don't like to be alone for long periods of time. Could your Bichon's unwanted behaviors be the result of separation anxiety? Consider hiring a dog walker to taking your Bichon to doggy daycare if there's no way to avoid leaving your Bichon home alone all day.

The definition of bad behavior will vary for every person as will the perceived severity of the behavior. Setting behavior expectations has been discussed throughout the book, and for good reason: it's the single best way to encourage your dog to behave. Without solid expectations your dog will not understand what is good or bad.

Dogs can be impulsive, so whether it is the remnants of last night's dinner calling to him from the garbage or the idea that chasing the cat will be fun, he will do what he wants. It's what you do in that situation that will define your dog's future behavior.

Bad behavior has a vast range, but some of the more minor offenses could include eating out of the garbage, chewing on furniture, shoes, or other belongings, barking excessively, digging in the yard, chasing other pets, and jumping on furniture or other people.

Major misbehavior would be showing aggression toward other animals or people, scavenging, and biting. These are behaviors that might be serious enough to warrant bringing in a professional, which is discussed later in this chapter.

Whether your dog is breaking small rules or large ones, it is possible to work to fix the behavior. It may take time and patience, but dogs, especially Bichons, are in the business of loving and impressing their people, so with some work and consistency, worst behaviors should be treatable.

Photo Courtesy of
Sheryn Turner

Finding the Root of the Problem

Sometimes, finding the root of the problem can be the hardest part of fixing behavior in dogs. It isn't always obvious and can be a mix of different reasons.

One of the most common reasons for bad behavior in dogs, especially minor bad behavior, is excess energy. When dogs are left to their own devices, such as when you're at work or even in a different part of your home, and they have a lot of energy, anything can happen. A lot of times chewing, barking, jumping, and chasing are just an excess of energy that your dog doesn't know how to release. Keeping your dog mentally and physically engaged throughout the day can be the key to avoiding trouble.

Another reason a dog might misbehave is separation anxiety, which is a very common issue among Bichons who are extremely attached to their owners. If your dog suffers from separation anxiety, he may become so distraught that he ruins your possessions or has accidents in the house.

If you adopted your dog and he has bad habits, then he likely was not trained well in his original home. Luna was abused by her first owners and as a result showed some food and toy aggression when we first got her. She would take a toy or bone and protect it instead of playing with it. It has taken us three years of consistent, patient training to mitigate the issue. Now if her instinct kicks in and she takes a toy to protect, she will willingly give it up in trade for her favorite treat.

Health issues can also cause bad behavior in dogs. Every dog will have a different reaction to health problems, but some could act out by showing aggression or growling. Sometimes your dog might not be able to control the issue. If he has a urinary tract infection or a problem with his digestive system, he might not have control of urination or defecation.

Though dogs will respond differently to health ailments, there are some consistent responses to certain health issues. If your dog gets injured, he will likely lick the area excessively and possibly even protect the area that is injured. One time, Luna sliced her paw on something. It wasn't really bleeding but she was obsessively licking her paw. She wouldn't stop and when we tried to look at it she would growl at us. We diffused the situation by giving her a lot of love and talking in a calming voice while petting her. One of us started looking at all of her paws so she didn't think we were going after her injury. We did the same thing for each paw and she finally let us touch the injured one. This is a very common reaction for most dogs to have when they are injured.

Vets are a great resource and a quick checkup is usually all it takes to determine if the bad behavior is a health issue or behavioral. Once you have ruled out illness or injury, you can then work through the behavioral side of the problem.

Bad Behavior Prevention

If you have consulted a vet and determined that your dog's bad behavior is in fact a behavioral problem, then you can start to dissect what might be causing the issue. One of the biggest reasons a dog might misbehave is simply having too much energy. If you leave your dog at home for long periods of time, such as when you are at work, and your dog is being destructive or having accidents, it's very likely that he's bored.

If your dog has too much energy, taking him for a long walk or even to a dog park in the morning could tire him out for at least part of the day.

There are also engaging toys you can purchase for your dog to play with throughout the day. They make puzzle toys and food-based toys which will engage your dog with a fun mental challenge. Designate toys that you will only give when you are gone or maybe rotate through a few toys.

Another option is to hire a dog walker for a mid-day walk. There are several apps where you can schedule dog walkers that have had background checks and you can pick the walker that fits your dog's personality best. There is also the old-fashioned neighborhood kid you could hire to take your dog for a walk while you are gone for work. This mid-day break is a great way to prevent a huge energy burst in the afternoon.

Doggy day care is always an option as well while you're at work, though it can get quite expensive. If your dog is social and loves other dogs, then this is a great option to keep him out of trouble during the day.

The best way to prevent bad behavior is to make sure all of your dog's needs are met and he is well exercised. Another key to preventing bad behavior is to have consistent expectations. If you don't want him on furniture, but you let him up on the couch sometimes and not others, this is very confusing and your dog won't know he's doing something wrong. While being consistent with your expectations can be hard, it can save a lot of headaches in the long run.

How to Properly Correct Your Dog

"Be patient and never scold your Bichon, instead always reward and praise good behavior."

Karen Graeber
Whitebred Bichons

Before you start the process of correcting your dog's bad behavior, it is important to note that it is exactly that, a process. The behavior won't stop overnight, and it might even take months, or as I found out, years before a behavior shifts completely. My dog was a special situation due to being abused by her first owner. For the average dog, trying to break a bad habit or change a behavior can take weeks to months.

Patience, consistency, and persistence are three key words when correcting bad behavior. If you exhibit those three traits while correcting your dog, eventually he will likely listen. It's important to note that a habit like begging for food can be hard to break but for most dogs, bad behavior can be curbed into good behavior.

Photo Courtesy of
Kathy Leavitt

It's important not to yell or scare your dog, as this could lead to more anxiety or bad behavior. Some dogs that have minor behavioral issues don't even know they're doing something wrong; they're just experiencing a strong emotion and instinctively responding to it.

When to Call a Professional

If your dog is deemed healthy by your vet and is still exhibiting exceedingly concerning behavior such as aggression or consistently going to the bathroom in the house, it's probably time to call a professional. A dog who is aggressive with other dogs and animals is a danger to them and himself. This doesn't necessarily mean the dog is a bad dog, just that something is wrong.

Animals are very sensitive to the environment around them, so even small changes might affect their behavior. If your dog is exhibiting potentially dangerous behavior due to anxiety or fear, calling in a dog behaviorist could have a life-changing impact.

Dog behaviorists are professionals who have a degree in behavioral science. In order for a dog behaviorist to be accredited they must have a doctorate degree in either behavioral science or veterinary medicine. They also must have professional experience in animal behavior. Similar to a professional dog trainer or even your vet, behaviorists have extensive knowledge and experience working with dogs.

If your dog suffers from severe separation anxiety, OCD, or is aggressive in any way, it might be time to call in a professional. Your vet is a great resource you can use to determine if you are on the fence about calling in a professional. They likely have dog behaviorists they can recommend as well.

Bichon Frise–Specific Bad Habits

As a breed, Bichons are extremely kind and love kids and other dogs. That being said, Bichons are notorious for having separation anxiety. They see themselves as an extension of their owner and never want to be apart from their family. Separation anxiety can be the root of destructive behavior, especially when you're not in the house.

Additionally, the "Bichon buzz" is just a fact of life. Your snuggly little fluff will get seemingly instant bursts of energy and this isn't bad behavior.

It's just a breed characteristic. As such, it's important to have engaging toys and space for your dog to run around your house.

Bichons will do nearly anything to please you. This also means they can get pretty easily distracted trying to impress you. In some dogs, this can lead to trouble potty training or learning basic commands. Just keep this in mind and practice a little extra patience if your dog is struggling to master a command or behavior. He's probably just trying to show you how much he loves you and get back to your side as quickly as possible!

Photo Courtesy of Pam Volkert

CHAPTER 13
Traveling with Your Bichon Frise

Bichons typically make wonderful travel companions as long as they have access to their owners. That said, with traveling in general, early exposure is key to success, along with being prepared. Introduce your Bichon to car rides and travel opportunities at an early age.

Photo Courtesy of
Brittany Lindley

Choosing a Carrier

There are many carriers available for short distances. Two popular options are hard plastic travel crates and soft-sided carriers. Both of these have pros and cons.

A hard travel crate is made of strong, durable plastic that is quite difficult for a Bichon to damage. Additionally, a travel crate is made of two halves, and can be easily taken apart when not in use, for storage, or to deep clean it. It can be wiped out with soap and water or hosed out for larger messes. If you plan to fly with your Bichon eventually, it would be wise to choose a travel crate that meets airline restrictions—typically, soft carriers are used for in-cabin travel and hard crates are required for travel in cargo. Call airlines to get an idea of what these restrictions are. To make the plastic crate more comfortable, provide a bed that fits nicely inside. You can also purchase clip-on food and water bowls, so your Bichon has full access to both while traveling.

Another popular option is a soft-sided travel carrier. These carriers have frames that are usually made of steel or aluminum tubes. The fabric tends to be water resistant and the windows are made of mesh for viewing and ventilation. These carriers often have handles and are similar to a large tote bag, but more structured. While these carriers are less durable than their plastic counterparts, they are easy to fold and store, and more flexible, making fitting them under a seat on a plane possible. Most travel crates can be strapped into a seat belt, making them much more stable and secure for your Bichon.

To choose the proper size of carrier for your Bichon, consider these three things: current and projected full size of the dog, the most common ways you will use the carrier, and the ultimate needs of your pet. If you are flying with your pet, he must have clearance for his head and be able to completely turn around, stand, and lie down. If your Bichon is traveling on a plane, but in cargo, he must have a plastic crate with food and water bowls attached to the door. If you will be crate training your pup, using the same plastic crate during that time can be cost effective. You can choose a crate or carrier that is ideal for the projected full size of your Bichon and then block off a portion of it for your young puppy. Safety, comfort, and value should all be considered. Beginning your search online can be very useful so you can read customer reviews. But don't underestimate the value of taking your Bichon to the pet store to see and feel your options before committing. Due to the small size of the breed, having more than one type of carrier may be a good solution for your various travel needs.

Car Restraints

Most Bichons are always up for a car ride! But as is true for any member of your family, safety is essential. There are two main types of restraints you can use to keep your pup safe.

Headrest restraints

Headrest restraints attach to the space between your car's headrest and the seat back. This option allows the strap to hang down the center of the seat, which is optimal for keeping your Bichon in the center of the seat. The strap that attaches to your dog's harness is adjustable in length so you can provide enough slack for your dog to be comfortable and not choking, while also keeping him from roaming onto your console or into your lap.

Seat belt restraints

The seat belt restraint is simply a strap or cord that attaches to the harness and then clicks into the seat belt receiver, just like a standard seatbelt. The restraint is usually an adjustable nylon strap with a carabiner or thumb hook to attach to the harness. There are also bungee-style options that allow your Bichon a bit more mobility and a coated steel cord option (similar to a bike lock) that is designed for dogs who chew. When it comes to bungee cords, you'll need to choose the correct size because they're not adjustable. These cords must be used in the back seat and are attached to the latch or bracket used to install child seats.

The Danger of Airbags

Airbags can be dangerous for dogs because of the force with which they deploy. If your Bichon will be riding in a seat with front or side airbags, try to position the dog as far away from the airbags as possible. To avoid airbags completely, use a travel carrier or have your dog travel on the floorboards of your vehicle. You should always check the vehicle's specifics to determine the safest place for your Bichon based on airbag placement.

Photo Courtesy of Kathy Leavitt

Never allow your Bichon to travel in the bed of a truck because a sudden stop or a fender bender could cause injury or death. I have also seen a dog that was tethered into the truck bed almost choke to death when it tried to jump out of the truck while it was still moving. Also remember that your pet needs good air ventilation so make sure that the vehicle vents can effectively cool your dog, and keep the crate covered if there is direct sun. Sadly, dogs have died while in air-conditioned vehicles because the sun was directly on them or because the vents could not adequately cool them. Hatchbacks, vans, and sport utility vehicles have the advantage of roomy trunk space that is ideal for travel carriers, but as always, ensure that the temperature and ventilation is comfortable and safe for your Bichon. Check on him often and provide water and stretching breaks often as well.

Preparing Your Bichon for the Road

With proper preparation, most Bichons will love riding along with their family! If you are not sure if your Bichon will like riding in the car, start with a short trip with a positive destination like the park or anywhere where your dog can walk and sniff. Exploring is very rewarding for Bichons. They are very social, making checking out new scenery a true joy for them. Make sure that your Bichon does not associate the car with going to the veterinarian only. Ideally, take your dog on fun car trips more often than you do on negative trips.

With young or nervous Bichons, it is wise to cover your seats in case of car sickness or nervous bowel movements. Use a towel, a blanket, or a seat protector under the carrier or directly under your pet. A bed or soft blanket will likely make your dog more comfortable as well.

Stress is the primary contributing factor to dogs who experience motion sickness. But in young dogs, motion sickness can simply be the result of an as-yet underdeveloped inner ear structure which establishes their feeling of balance. If your pup has experienced motion sickness in the car before, he may develop a fear of riding and extra patience and preparedness will be essential to help him re-acclimate to riding comfortably.

If your Bichon is prone to motion sickness, consider essential oils like lavender or peppermint, calming treats, CBD oil or treats, or a prescription medicine from your veterinarian. Make sure to follow the dosing instructions and to give the medicine in plenty of time to take effect before leaving home

Make sure your Bichon has plenty of time to potty before hitting the road. Some pups will not potty in strange places so it's highly important to give them more than enough time to do their business in the comfort of their

Photo Courtesy of
Blanca Soto

usual spot. Feed your dog several hours in advance to give him time to digest his food completely. Some Bichons, however, will need a small bit of food in their bellies to prevent motion sickness. You will have to observe your Bichon to see what works. Either way, your dog should be well hydrated at all times.

Ensure the temperature is comfortable in the vehicle. Sometimes your Bichon will prefer the windows down for fresh air, over having the air conditioning. Just make sure he is completely secure so there is no chance that he can jump out of the window. You can also roll the window down just a few inches so your pup can enjoy the fresh air safely.

When taking your Bichon on the road with you, make sure that you pack water, water and food bowls, food for longer drives, toys, chewables like hard bones or treat-filled rubber toys, and all of the safety gear we discussed earlier. It is convenient to bring a small cooler or thermos of ice chips to give your pup if stopping for water often is not realistic or if having a water bowl in the car is messy. You can also buy water bottles like rabbits use and travel bottles that have a basin that the water flows into making it easy for pets to drink on the go. If you like to feed your Bichon fresh produce or meat as a treat, consider a small insulated lunch bag or a backpack cooler. You and your Bichon can share these and each have a variety of tasty and healthy treats for the road.

Early riding success can set the stage for many years of enjoyable car rides and road trips for you and your furry best friend!

Flying and Hotel Stays

"They can get very anxious when left alone in a strange place, and will bark if left in a hotel room by themselves."

Jeanette Neagu
Takoda Dogs

With Bichons' smaller size, traveling is far easier than with larger dog breeds. As a result, there are many vacation options for you and your Bichon family. Here are a few of the primary considerations when planning a Bichon-friendly vacation: Where are we going? How will we get there? Where will we stay? What is our strategy? How will we play?

Photo Courtesy of
Susan Snow

If spending the maximum amount of time with your Bichon is your goal, you must first consider the city you will choose as your destination. There are places that are simply more inherently dog friendly. Coastal areas tend to have a more-dog friendly culture. In these locations, you will see more dogs on leashes, in pet carriers, or even in strollers. Also, in these areas, more restaurants will allow dogs inside, or will at least have outdoor seating for you and your pup. Lake cities like Chicago also rate high on the dog-friendly city list, as well as Vegas, Tucson, and New York (yes, it's coastal though not what we usually picture when we think of the beach). Whether you want to hit the big city, visit the desert, climb a mountain, or search for shells, there is a great destination ready to welcome you and your Bichon.

Vacations with pets require much more planning. If you are a spur of the moment person, visit places that you know well and where you are confident taking your dog. If you are not sure, then careful planning is required to ensure that the trip goes off without a hitch.

Fly Away with Me

The pin is on the map. Now that you know where you are headed, if you have decided that flying is part of your travel plans, now it is time to choose an airline and plan your trip. As you know, not all airlines allow pets in the cabin. Important note: most international flights are much stricter about allowing pets on board. You will have to not only check on the airline's policy, but also the policies and laws of the country you are traveling to. For this reason, we will focus on domestic travel only.

First, find out which airlines will allow you to bring your Bichon on board with you. Check all of their requirements for size and weight to make sure your Bichon falls within the guidelines. If you are not 100% sure, don't wing it (pun intended). Call the airline and verify their policy. You don't want to show up with your luggage and an excited pup just to be sent home.

Before booking your flight, make sure that any pet fees are not cost prohibitive. Also check

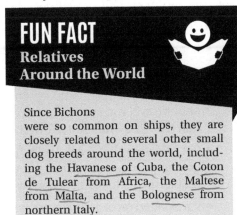

FUN FACT
Relatives Around the World

Since Bichons were so common on ships, they are closely related to several other small dog breeds around the world, including the Havanese of Cuba, the Coton de Tulear from Africa, the Maltese from Malta, and the Bolognese from northern Italy.

pet fee cancelation policy. This is often different from an airline's ticket cancelation policy. Usually you will have to call the airline directly to schedule your pet's flight and then pay the fee over the phone or at the counter when you arrive at the airport to check in. If you have more than one Bichon or pet, find out how many each person can bring and how many you can put in each carrier. Typically, each person can bring one carrier and each carrier can have up to two pets. Service animals usually do not count against your total.

Next, choose a dog carrier that meets an airline's size requirements. Measure your carrier carefully to double check. You don't want to leave anything to chance. The carriers can be hard or soft (see the previous section on hard vs. soft carriers when it comes to cabin vs. cargo travel), must be vented, and must allow room for the pet to stand and turn around easily. You can get carriers with shoulder straps, as backpacks, or even as rolling bags. Remember that most airlines will count a carrier as a carry-on bag, thus reducing the number of carry-ons you can bring for yourself. Airlines often sell pet carriers. You can order these directly from their website and have them shipped to your home in advance of your flight.

Always introduce your Bichon to the carrier well in advance to allow him to get used to being in it. Let him go in and out, exploring the new space at will. Set the carrier next to you on the couch or by your feet while you work. Feed your Bichon in it at times. Put his favorite toys and blankets inside. Make this his favorite new cozy spot if possible. Make being in it a treat! This will make the flight much easier for you and your Bichon!

Flying with Your Bichon

Now that you have planned your flight carefully, it's time to pack. The following are items you should always take with you when you travel:

- Travel crate.

- Food and water bowls (metal or plastic).

- Food and treats.

- Medication, supplements, essential oil, etc. Consult your veterinarian about travel medications and read your airline's policy on pet sedation (which is often not allowed).

- Put cold items in a small cooler bag. Wait to purchase a bottle of water until after you have passed through security. Check with your airline's requirements for coolers and for bringing prepared food onboard.

- Vaccination records (these are not always required but are very wise to have on hand.) You can also keep these on your smartphone or tablet.

- Collar, harness, and leash.
- Comfort items: small blanket, toys, bones, etc.
- Wet wipes and plastic storage bags, just in case of an accident.
- You may be allowed to bring an additional crate or pet stroller that can be checked with your checked luggage. There may or may not be a charge for this.

Additionally, when making your travel plans:

- **Plan for comfort.** Allow your Bichon ample opportunity to eat, drink, and potty at home and near the airport if possible. There are places to also walk your pet in airports and let him relieve himself.
- **Follow the rules.** While in the airport, keep your Bichon in the carrier at all times and on a leash if in the designated area for dog walking.
- **Print and pay.** Print your boarding pass and then go directly to the airline counter to check your dog in and pay related fees.
- **Pass through security.** You will have to follow all of the regular security policies plus take your Bichon through security too. Expect to have to remove him from his carrier so it can go through the X-ray conveyer belt. You will then have to carry your pet through the personal security area, and he will be scanned along with you. After you both pass through security, you can (and must) put him back in his carrier.

Pro Tip

Plan for success by removing your belt and jacket, wearing slip-on shoes, and packing your personal liquids in your checked luggage so you have less to handle.

- **Plan to potty.** Before heading to your boarding gate, take your pup to the dog walking area for a quick tinkle. Better there than in your pet's fresh new carrier!
- **Prepare to board.** Keep your pet secure in his carrier but make sure you pet him, giving him lots of loving encouragement. This is a great time to add a drop or two of calming essential oils or to offer your dog's favorite bone. Stay calm and so will he. Do not expect to board early unless you have preferred boarding or have a service animal.
- **Prepare for flight.** Put your personal effects overhead and place your pet under the seat in front of you. Give him a small dish and water, and

food. You will probably not be able to hold your pet during flight. If you have the go-ahead to do so, then enjoy! But don't expect it.

- **Prepare for landing.** You did it! You successfully maneuvered your first airborne adventure with your sweet pup! Take him to potty and then celebrate!

Flying with your Bichon the first time might not be easy, but with careful planning, it should not be terribly difficult. Prepare for issues and you will plan for success. Plan for messes and you won't be surprised. Plan for traffic so you won't be late. And give yourself a lot of extra time. Your efforts will be totally worth it.

Where to stay? Hotels, house sharing, and more

There are more options than ever for staying and playing with your favorite little four-legged pal. These include cabins, hotels, rental properties, house sharing (like Airbnb), and more.

Here are some special considerations when choosing pet-friendly accommodations:

- **Consider choosing a ground floor or lower floor room** to make potty breaks easier.
- **Consider a suite.** This will allow your pup more room to run and play inside.
- **Choose a location with ample green space.** House sharing is a wonderful choice, especially if it offers a fenced in yard. When choosing a hotel or an urban location, look at the satellite view (like Google Earth) to see where the greenspace, or a nearby dog park, is located.
- **Look at online reviews.** Not all dog-friendly options are ideal. Check for amenities, cleanliness, and friendliness of staff.
- **Speaking of amenities,** ask if they have any dog services like dog walking while you are sightseeing.
- **Ask about other pets.** If you are house sharing, ask about any pets already in the home and make sure to discuss the compatibility of your pets. Also ask about house policies such as if pets are allowed on the furniture. Be considerate and clean up all of your pet's indoor and outdoor messes completely and don't use the home's personal kitchenware to feed your dog.

Additionally, make sure you:

- **Pay attention to your surroundings.** Nearby roads can be dangerous. Always take your dog out on a leash and be very clear with children about potential hazards to your pup.

- **Ask for a non-smoking room or location.** Your Bichon does not need to be exposed to secondhand smoke.

- **If your dog is a barker, or fearful of people, put the do not disturb sign on the door** to keep housekeeping away while you are away. Also consider putting a blanket over your pup's crate while you are not in the hotel or house.

- **Check the policies about crating and leaving pets in the room** while you are away. Most hotels expect animals to be crated, while others don't allow dogs to be left behind at all. If this is the case, look for a nearby pet spa or daycare so your Bichon can get groomed or play while you are out and about.

More than likely you will be expected to sign a pet agreement and pay a pet deposit and/or cleaning fee. You will be expected to follow all of the pet policies and may be asked to remove your pet if noise complaints are received. If you are highly concerned about your Bichon's barking, you need to have a plan in place to limit your dog's barking such as having them wear a thunder shirt, using a white noise machine, offering a treat-filled hard rubber chew toy, and maybe even using a calming product such as chewable calming treats. At the very least, leave the TV on for your Bichon and leave a clothing item that smells like you. This may offer enough reassurance to your Bichon so you can be gone a couple of hours.

Tips and Tricks for Traveling

Traveling with your Bichon is similar to traveling with a child. Preparation is key! Prepare for the best. Prepare for things to go wrong. Prepare for a great time! Here are some travel tips to make traveling easy and fun:

- Make sure your dog is microchipped and that his collar fits properly and won't come off easily. Have your contact information stitched onto the collar. If you will be stopping at picnic tables or staying at an RV park, bring a tie out so your Bichon can safely roam within a few feet while you set up lunch.

- Bring toys that your dog likes, such as a special bone or antler, even a movie that he likes. Pack a Frisbee, tennis ball, or a squeak toy to play with in the car or when you pull over.

- Pack carrots, apple slices, blueberries, jerky, chunks of sweet potatoes, etc. Bring ice cubes or ice chips or get some from the soda fountain section at a fast food restaurant or gas station.

- Take your dog on a big walk before you leave or to their favorite dog daycare the day before you leave. Find a park or dog park along your route and enjoy a break together. A tired dog is a relaxed dog.
- Get ready for messes. There will be messes. Have a cleaning supply bag with paper towels, cleaning wipes, small trash bags, disinfectant spray and/or air freshener, baking soda (to absorb urine), and a large towel so no one has to sit in any damp spots.
- Bring alcohol swabs, ointment, scissors, tweezers, and bandages in case of an injury.
- An upset tummy is the most likely ailment your pup will experience. Bring a couple of peppermints and give your pup small pieces as needed to settle his tummy. Benadryl can help with upset tummies too. The rule of thumb is one milligram of Benadryl per pound that your dog weighs. Also, CBD oil and treats have become a very popular way to calm your pup while traveling. When in doubt about motion sickness, talk to your vet.
- Play good tunes! Fun music makes for a fun trip. If your dog prefers classical, throw on some Beethoven. You can create a playlist in advance and download it, especially if you will be traveling through the mountains where reception is very spotty.

The best travel tip is to create memories! Take lots of pictures with your Bichon, plan to get a souvenir for him in special locations, take your time and try to enjoy the journey and not just rush to the destination. After all, you have the privilege of being with your road dog! Enjoy it!

Boarding vs. Hiring a Sitter

Sometimes, taking your dog along on a trip is just not the best idea. Fortunately, there are excellent options for boarding or hiring care for your Bichon while you are away. It is important to know that Bichons are very attached to their owners. Separation anxiety is common in the breed but with proper care, your Bichon can actually have his own vacation while you are away. When you find the right care provider for your Bichon, you will know because you will actually be able to relax and enjoy your time away, focus on your business trip, or handle family affairs without constantly worrying about your pet.

Bichons are extremely social and active! If you are away, it is important that they have plenty of human contact, and if possible, dog interaction as well. Whether you choose to keep your dog at home or at a facility, socialization should be one of your primary concerns.

Pros and Cons of Hiring a Sitter

PROS

- Your pet gets to stay at home. This is good because he will be confident in his surroundings. His routine should be relatively similar to what it is when you are home.

- Your Bichon does not have to get used to new animals or be exposed to potential illness. There isn't a risk of injury from an aggressive dog.

- If you have a security system, video cameras, a video camera doorbell, or other security options in your home, you can keep an eye on the care your dog is receiving.

- The pet sitter can help with small tasks at your home while you are away.

CONS

- Unless the pet sitter is there as often as you would normally be, your pet may get bored, restless, or anxious.

- Your pet may have accidents in your home that he might not have if you were home. This is not necessarily due to poor care from the pet sitter. Dogs, especially Bichons, can act differently when their owners are away. This is a greater risk if your Bichon is not kennel trained.

- Not all pet sitters are reliable. Sometimes they run late or forget to show up. You also have to consider the safety and security of your home. Even pet sitters whom I have hired and trusted immensely have made poor choices that affected the safety of my pets and my home. I have come home to considerable damage due to my dogs being neglected. They have had accidents, chewed up remote controls, and even chewed on the drywall!

- Pet sitters are not always aware of the ways your pets can get out. If you choose to use a pet sitter, be very clear about any possible ways your pet may try to escape. It's not uncommon to see posts on social media about dogs that get out and run away while the pet sitter was caring for them.

Hiring a Pet Sitter

If you decide that hiring a pet sitter is best for your Bichon, be sure to get references from the pet sitter's other clients. Invite the sitter over to show them around your home and to introduce them to your Bichon. If your pet is not comfortable with them, keep looking. If your Bichon does not care for them, it does not mean that they are a bad person, but it could mean that they are not a good fit for your Bichon, and that's okay. Don't force it. Keep interviewing until you find a well-qualified fit that your Bichon takes to.

If your Bichon avidly barks and backs up and does not want to be touched, do not force the interaction. Let your Bichon take the lead, allowing him to approach the sitter if and when he is ready. Ask the sitter not to pick up your Bichon right away as some Bichons feel out of control and scared when strangers do this. If the Bichon wants more of the sitter's attention, he will show it by sitting near, or even on, the sitter. This is a great sign! My Bichon runs to certain people and clamors for their affection. This makes me feel amazing because I want him to have other people that he feels safe with besides just me and my family. I don't want him to be terrified if I am away any more than I want my child to be scared when he is at school or at a friend's house.

Here are some things you should tell and show your sitter:
- Your pet's routine and where all of his belongings are located.
- Where your pets can go and cannot go in the house and outside.
- Any habits you are working to deter in your pet. Also show the sitter any commands you are working on with your pet.
- Feeding times and amounts.
- Location of medications and instructions.
- Location of first aid supplies.
- Emergency contact and veterinary information.
- Location of keypads, alarms, keys, etc.
- Where to put your mail or packages.
- Where to put pet waste like potty pads and how to clean messes if your pet has an accident.
- Where to put the trash can if the trash service comes while you are away.
- Anything else important for your pet or your home.

- Discuss pay in detail. Are you paying them per visit or a flat rate? When will they get paid? I suggest paying them a deposit to book the job, so they take the booking seriously, and then pay them the remaining balance due at the end.

- I strongly recommend creating a master calendar of what they should do and when they should visit during the time you will be gone as well as a daily schedule of needed times for caring for your pets. If your instructions are long or complicated, consider making a checklist for them to review daily.

- If you would like them to do any cleaning, such as vacuuming, before you get home from your trip, make sure to request this when you are reviewing the expectations of the job. Try to eliminate the possibility of surprises in duties so that the sitter doesn't feel taken advantage of by last-minute requests.

- Ask your potential sitter for references (if they were not already referred by someone you know and trust) and ask them how they have previously handled separation anxiety, emergencies, health concerns, damaged property, or any other issue of concern to you.

Overnight Sitters

You may choose to have your pet sitter sleep in your home. This is particularly helpful if you have a pet with a very rigid schedule or who takes meds at a set time late in the evening or early in the morning. An overnight sitter may also be a good fit for you if your Bichon is used to sleeping in the bed with you. If you would like the sitter to allow the dog to sleep in the bed with him or her, make sure to express this and make sure that they are comfortable with those arrangements. If you have a young dog who is still potty training, or a dog who simply needs to be let out during the night, discuss this in detail with the sitter. Not all sitters will be able to get up in the middle of the night, especially if they have other commitments like work or school in the morning.

If you do hire a sitter to stay in your home, there are a few more details to discuss:

- What time do they need to be in for the night to stay with the dogs, and until what time in the morning?

- Who they can have over to the home with them?

- Who to call if there's an emergency in the middle of the night?

- What food they are welcome to eat.

- Where to find extra linens for themselves.

- Anything that you suggest that they bring from home (I usually suggest that they bring their favorite pillows since I know that I sleep better with my own pillow.)

- The location of video cameras in your home. You may find it reassuring to know that you can check on your dogs at any time via your home cameras. I choose to tell my house sitters where the cameras are located to protect their personal privacy. I would never want to make a sitter feel uncomfortable by not giving them a heads-up so they can speak and dress appropriately while in my home. And I would never eavesdrop on their phone conversations. I find that this is important in creating mutual trust and respect.

A few notes about hiring a sitter who is under the age of 18 (or 21 concerning alcohol):

- Be sure to receive permission from their parents before you hire them.

- Remove alcohol and medications from your home that could pose a risk to them.

- Consider allowing them to have a friend or sibling stay the night with them. When I use a sitter who is younger, I always offer to allow them to have someone stay with them that their parents would also approve of.

- Make sure that they can drive, and if they can't, speak with their parents directly about transportation of the sitter and of your pets in case of an emergency.

- Also consider asking a friend or neighbor to check in at your home from time to time to make sure that everything is running smoothly with the sitter and your pets.

Once you find a great sitter, remember to pay them fairly so that they will continue to want to work for you. Also remember that cheaper is not always better. Sitters with solid references will likely charge more than those without experience, but there is peace of mind that comes with the reputation for high quality care.

Continue to expect quality care from your sitter moving forward. If your sitter lapses in their care of your pet, discuss it with them. If you feel that the mistake was too great to fully trust them again, then begin looking for a new sitter long before your next trip. And if you ever sense that your Bichon is no longer comfortable with the sitter, find a new one, even if you can't pinpoint the source of your dog's feelings.

Pro and Cons of Using a Boarding Facility (Kennel)

Boarding facilities, also known as "kennels," come in all shapes and sizes. Some are very plush, with salon services and a spa feel. Some have private rooms, flat-screen TVs, and tuck-in services. Others are activity- and play-centered with playgrounds and obstacle courses. Some are simply equipped with kennels or runs and provide the basics in care without any extras.

Boarding Facility (Kennel)

PROS	CONS
• Many kennels take the dogs out for fresh air, socialization, and playtime activities. Exercise is one of the best ways to decrease anxiety and boredom in dogs. And Bichons especially need exercise and stimulation!	• Some kennels only let the dogs out twice a day.
• Kennel staff typically know first aid, safety, and CPR for animals.	• Many kennels are only staffed part of the day.
• Your Bichon may have the opportunity to make new friends through supervised playgroups that are tailored to your pet's size and play style.	• Hands-on interaction between the dogs and staff varies by facility.
• Many kennels offer baths or grooming.	
• Some kennels offer video viewing of your dog's room.	

Before selecting a facility, call ahead to schedule a meet-and-greet or a tour. Bring your pet if possible, to gauge his comfort level while there and to observe how the staff interacts with your Bichon. Here are some questions you should ask:

- What does a typical daily schedule look like?
- How many potty breaks will my dog get?

- Will my dog play with other dogs? How do you assess each dog for compatibility?

- How do you manage separation anxiety in pets?

- Do you offer the type of feeding, medical care, and medication administration my pet needs?

- Is there a vet or vet tech onsite? If not, what kind of training does the staff have?

- What activities are included?

- How often will I receive updates?

- Will you provide any photo updates?

- What is your emergency protocol if my Bichon becomes ill or gets injured? Who is financially responsible? How will you make decisions concerning my dog if I cannot be reached?

- How do you keep the dogs separate and secure when needed?

- Is anyone onsite overnight?

- Can I see where my Bichon will eat, sleep, potty, and play?

Photo Courtesy of Pat Rossi

Also discuss your Bichon's fears, preferences, allergies, grooming needs, and more. Ask about available add-ons that may help your Bichon be more comfortable during his stay.

It is important to read reviews about a boarding facility before taking your Bichon there and to ask for references if you are new to the area. If you choose a facility and you have concerns during or after a stay, ask questions. Ask for a report card of each stay. And always pay attention to your Bichon's verbal and non-verbal communication when you pick him up. Is he happy, excited, and joyfully barking with his tail wagging? Or does he seem scared? Some hesitation may be normal for your pet, but the photo updates, and how your Bichon acts when you pick him up from boarding, are all clues as to how he feels about his time at the kennel.

The Bottom Line for Choosing Pet Care

There's no one-size-fits-all approach to choosing accommodations for your Bichon. Consider the health, activity level, anxiety level, need for socialization, personality, emotional needs, and history of your Bichon before making a decision. Ultimately you have to follow your gut. You are your dog's parent, advocate, and protector. A loving caregiver who understands how emotionally sensitive Bichons are is essential. While Bichons typically love playful activity with other dogs, they do not want to be yelled at or intimidated. They also desperately crave human connection. A facility that requires your Bichon to stay in a kennel most of the day is not the best fit for your pet. Look for care that is a balance of exercise, human attention, socialization, and comfort. Your Bichon will thank you with lots of sweet kisses!

CHAPTER 14
Nutrition

The Importance of Good Diet

Proper nutrition is important with any breed or mixed breed of dog. The Bichon, however, is particularly sensitive to different food types. Bichons are very active and energetic dogs that require high quality nutrition to support their active lifestyle. Additionally, Bichons are prone to skin allergies and bladder issues that can be deeply affected by their diet. For this reason, it is essential to choose foods that use high quality ingredients and carefully balance proteins, fat, carbohydrates, fiber, vitamins, and minerals.

Photo Courtesy of
Cindy Gelnette

The Best Ingredients for Your Bichon

Proteins

Proteins are the building blocks of your Bichon's diet. They include fish, turkey, chicken, duck, beef, lamb, and liver. Choosing a protein (or combination of proteins) is based on personal preference, your budget, your dog's taste preference, and your dog's particular health needs. Some Bichons can develop allergies to particular proteins.

Grains

Grains in your dog's diet could include brown rice, corn, wheat, oats, quinoa, barley, etc. When choosing grain ingredients, choose high quality grains, avoiding corn as a primary ingredient. Ingredients are listed in order of prominence on dog food packaging, so choose food that begins with your preferred protein and which is followed by grains like brown rice and barley.

HELPFUL TIP
Allergies

Bichons are prone to allergies, and your Bichon may struggle with food allergies. If your Bichon seems extra itchy, try putting him on a grain-free, limited-ingredient food, preferably with a unique protein (something other than beef or chicken). Change won't happen overnight, but a diet change could make a big difference with a little time if your Bichon has food allergies.

Vegetables and Fruits

Vegetables and fruits are a great source of vitamins and minerals for your Bichon and help provide improved flavor. Not all plant-based ingredients are safe either as an ingredient or a snack.

Foods You Should Never Feed Your Bichon (Or Any Dog)

- Onions
- Garlic
- Chives
- Grapes and raisins
- Cherries (they naturally contain cyanide)
- Chocolate
- Anything with caffeine
- Anything with alcohol

- Artificial sweeteners (be careful not to leave protein bars, candy, and gum lying around). Some of these sweeteners include:
  - Xylitol
  - Sugar alcohols
  - Aspartame
  - Saccharin
  - Sucralose
  - Sorbitol
  - Maltitol
  - Splenda
  - Stevia
- Tree nuts (including nut butters that contain tree nuts like almond butter) *no pistachio!*
- Yeast dough (raw, unbaked dough because it is still expanding)
- High-sodium snacks
- Cooked bones or large quantities of meat fat
- Undercooked meats
- Raw eggs (your veterinarian may recommend an occasional raw egg, but giving them often can cause issues)

- Citrus fruit
- Avocados
- Mushrooms
- Coconut water (go easy on coconut oil if you choose to use it)
- Dairy (small amounts of plain Greek yogurt is okay but make sure there isn't any artificial sweetener in it)

On a side note, if you would like to use essential oils on or near your pet, check with your vet. Even without being ingested, oils like cinnamon, citrus, and types of pine can be very dangerous to your Bichon's health.

Acceptable Foods to Feed Your Bichon

- Apple slices (no core)
- Bananas (limit quantity because of the high sugar content)
- Blueberries (fresh or frozen)
- Brussels sprouts and cabbage (both are safe, but both can cause gas)
- Cantaloupe (limit for dogs with diabetes)
- Carrots
- Celery
- Cranberries (fresh or dry)
- Green beans (fresh or frozen)
- Mango (skin removed)
- Peaches (toss the pit; it contains cyanide)
- Pears (fresh, no seeds or core)
- Peas (fresh or frozen)
- Pineapple
- Pumpkin (fresh or canned, plain, no sugar or spices)
- Raspberries (limited quantity as they contain trace amounts of Xylitol)
- Sweet potatoes
- Strawberries
- Watermelon

Different Types of Commercial Food

"I recommend using a high quality food along with vitamin and pro-biotic supplements like Missing Link. I have also always given Cranberry Relief to support a proper PH balance in their urine."

Betsy Savage
Dazzling Bichons

If you ask 50 people what you should feed your Bichon, you will likely get 50 different answers. Everyone has a different take on what proper nutrition for a Bichon means, just like we all have different views on what to put into our own bodies. If you choose to use commercial foods, you are in the majority of Americans who find that buying food, rather than making it, is a huge time saver.

Is commercial dog food good enough for your Bichon? Typically, yes. Most dog food companies use ethical and precise practices to manufacture your pet's food. They spend a lot of money on research and development to determine the best ingredients (or reasonably good ingredients) for their products.

It's our job as consumers to determine which packaged food is right for our pets, just like we need to read labels on all packaged food that we buy. Check every package for any known allergens or ingredients you want to avoid. Don't just look at the front of the bag. The bag might say "lamb and lentils," but it may also include chicken and cornmeal. Just because the bag contains what the label reads, doesn't mean it contains only the ingredients you desire and none of the ingredients you are trying to avoid. Make no assumptions. If the label reads "lamb" it should contain 70% lamb or more. If it is called something like "lamb supper," it is legally required to have at least 10% lamb. It the label reads, "with lamb," it is only required to have 3% of lamb.

Types of commercial dog food include dry kibble, canned wet food, freeze dried "raw" food, fresh refrigerated food, and even meal delivery services that send meals tailored to your pet's dietary needs directly to your doorstep. The dog food business is booming!

Here are some pros and cons of each type of dog food, as well as what to look for and what to avoid:

144

Kibble (Dry Food)

PROS

Open the bag and pour. It does not get any easier. And most reputable dog food brands manufacture kibble that contains not only good ingredients but also vitamins and minerals your dog needs. Since Bichons can be prone to dental problems, hard kibble is a good choice for removing plaque from their teeth as they chew. It's also easy to store, lasts the longest of all the food types, and travels extremely well.

CONS

Dogs can get bored with kibble from time to time (especially if they also get human food). Dog food could contain allergens that may upset your dog's digestion or irritate his skin. Dry food is only about 10% water, and your pet requires more in the way of moisture (in addition to the fresh drinking water supply he should always have available). You can also add water to dry food to make it soft when needed, or to make it seem more appealing to your dog, because wet food has a stronger smell than dry food.

What to look for:

Ingredients you recognize, protein at the top of the list and whole proteins like chicken or fish before you see support proteins like "chicken meal."

High quality grains, vegetables, and maybe even fruit.

Check that any kibble you purchase contains the following wording: "(Dog food name) is formulated to meet the nutritional levels established by the AAFCO Dog Food Nutrient Profiles."

Look for dry food that has kibble small enough for your Bichon's small mouth. There are even breed-specific dog foods that are designed to meet the unique dietary needs of the Bichon.

Ultimately, your dog needs to enjoy the food. It won't do you or your pup any good if it just sits in the pantry.

What to avoid:

High corn content

Any food that is expired or close to expiring

Any food bags that look damaged or tampered with

If you open a bag and the odor or color is different than what you are used to, contact the food company right away to let them know. Do not feed it to your dog. If you are at all concerned about the quality of the food, return it to the store.

Canned and Wet Packaged Food

PROS	CONS
Canned food is a great resource for a picky eater and can be combined with kibble to create a well-balanced meal that is affordable and pleasing to your dog. Canned food is also great for hiding medicine for dogs who are hard to medicate. Many tablets can be crushed before mixing it into the wet food, so your dog won't just eat around the pill (yes, it happens). Make sure that the pill is safe to crush and never open a capsule and pour it into the food without speaking to the doctor first. Some capsules need to be taken whole.	Once a dog gets used to eating canned food, it can be challenging to switch him back to kibble. Canned food can also be more expensive when looking at the overall serving size and price per meal. Canned food also does nothing to help scrub your Bichon's teeth. If you choose a wet only diet for your pet, make sure you regularly brush your dog's teeth and also offer your Bichon hard snacks like apple slices, carrot sticks, and celery.

What to look for:

Look for healthy ingredients that match the nutrition goals that you and your Bichon's vet have established.

What to avoid:

Ingredients that seem foreign to you and which sound like a list of chemicals.

Cans that are too large for your pet to eat before they need to be tossed.

Damaged, dented, or bloated cans or packages.

Freeze Dried Raw Food

PROS	CONS

The ingredient list should be pretty short, easy to read, and full of ingredients that most humans would enjoy. Freeze dried food is ideally freeze dried at the height of freshness and should contain few to no preservatives. Freeze dried food is a great option for pet owners who would love to personally prepare food for their pets, but don't have the time or ability to do so. This food travels well and simply needs water added to it to make it ready to consume. The bag is extremely light because the water has been removed, and the package takes up very little space. Once the water is added, the food will expand 3-5 times its size. Freeze dried food looks and smells good (at least to me) and reminds me of Thanksgiving stuffing. Yum.

It is typically much more expensive than kibble or canned/packaged wet food. And expensive doesn't necessarily mean that your dog will like it better. Find out the store or website's return policy for opened dog food before you purchase it. It can be very frustrating to think you're providing a great meal for your dog, only to find out that he won't eat it.

What to look for:

👍 Ingredients which include fresh meats and ingredients that are high in fiber and omega-3 fatty acids, and possibly healthy additives like flaxseed.

👍 Colorful, fresh-smelling food. You should be able to visually discern some of the individual ingredients (both before and after water has been added). Ask your local pet store if they have samples available to try before you buy. Boutique pet stores are often more accommodating than large pet stores.

👍 Country of origin. Choose food made in the US, Canada, Australia, New Zealand, or Western Europe.

What to avoid:

⊘ Any food that is close to its expiration date, as freshness is the point of freeze-dried dog food. However, freeze-dried food has a very long shelf life so this should rarely be an issue.

⊘ Artificial colors, flavors, or additives

⊘ Packaging that is not airtight

Packaged Refrigerated Dog Food

PROS	CONS
This food is very convenient and requires little to no preparation. It often comes in rolls, or logs, of food that is a mixture of minced meat and vegetables. Simply cut off the end of the packaging and cut off a section of the log to cut up and give to your dog. It is easy to add to kibble and can be used to give your dog a pill that has been hidden inside.	Refrigerated and packaged food will be more expensive than kibble or canned food but may be less expensive than freeze-dried food. It will contain preservatives to keep it fresh for up to one week. The food can go bad and become dangerous for your pet. Make sure to wrap it up carefully after you open it and to write the date that you opened it on the package or wrapper. Keep it at eye level so it doesn't get lost in the fridge. This food is pricey enough that you won't want to waste it.

What to look for:

👍 A container or food roll that your pet can eat completely in under a week. Some packages can be frozen if unopened.

👍 Check the packaging before going overboard on sale items that will expire before your pet can finish them.

👍 Quality meats and produce, as well as fiber. ✓

What to avoid:

⊘ Packages that are damaged or pierced.

⊘ Don't serve any food that smells strange or that has a gray or green tint.

Don't allow choosing a dog food to overwhelm you. Choose food that you can afford, that you feel comfortable with, that supports your dog's lifestyle and ideal weight, and that your Bichon enjoys. Sometimes choosing food is a matter of trial and error. If you choose a food that your dog doesn't like, or which appears to cause gastrointestinal issues, skin problems, or other health concerns, speak with your vet and remember to always gradually switch foods (unless the doctor wants you to stop a certain food immediately.)

Weight Management

According to the AKC's description of the Bichon Frise, the standard size of the breed is between 12 and 18 pounds and 9.5 to 11.5 inches tall, and they have a life expectancy of 14-15 years. With this in mind, weight management is an important tool in helping your Bichon not just live longer but enjoy doing so.

Managing your Bichon's weight will help him feel better overall and allow him to better maintain a healthy weight. A healthy Bichon will have a slender but not skinny build. You should be able to easily feel his ribs while palpating them with light pressure. If you can easily see the ribs, then your dog is too thin. If you can't easily feel his ribs, he is probably overweight, and you should decrease his caloric intake. Begin by decreasing or cutting out treats and as always, do not allow your Bichon to consume fatty foods or sugary treats.

Avoid fast food items, especially deep-fried menu items that not only add weight but can contribute to diseases like pancreatitis. Bichons are at a higher risk of pancreatitis, thus being mindful of their nutrients and weight is very important. Being overweight will only increase your dog's risk of contracting the condition.

Calorie Needs by Age and Size

An average size adult Bichon will need about 500-525 calories a day. The food should be divided into two, meaning that each meal should be about 250-260 calories. Check the caloric content of any food you feed your Bichon.

Active Bichons can need up to 700 daily calories. This is recommended for dogs who are very active, playing and running regularly, or participating in dog shows. Sedentary dogs will use fewer calories and therefore should eat less to avoid becoming overweight.

Puppies have different needs because they are so small but grow so quickly. Puppies are also very active and have a need for more healthy fat to develop their brains and growing muscles. Choose foods that are designed specifically for puppies and follow the feeding guidelines on the packaging. Young puppies under six months old should eat three times a day. Give the final meal a few hours before bedtime to allow plenty of time for the pup to successfully potty outside. Do not give your puppy too many treats. Offer small treats or treats broken into small pieces as training rewards and avoid rich foods that you might occasionally give your adult dog.

For the majority of your dog's life, he will be considered an adult dog. During these years, you will want to offer the best quality, limited ingredient food that you are able to provide. Look for high quality ingredients that you recognize with limited fillers. The food supplier will tell you how much to feed your dog based on their weight. However, there are other considerations such as energy level and your dog's lifestyle. In short, it depends on how your Bichon spends his day.

If your Bichon is walking for just a few minutes a day, and spending most of his time relaxing, consider feeding him at the lower end of the suggested range to avoid making him become overweight. If your dog walks or runs a couple of miles a day, he will likely need more calories, and can be served a higher amount of kibble. If your dog is training for agility and running obstacle courses regularly, you will need to increase his calories even more. You may also want to consider offering him a high-performance dog food for athletic dogs. The packaging may use the words "high performance," "sport," or "high protein." Dogs who are very physically active need high protein, essential fatty acids, and complex carbohydrates for muscle recovery. If they are extremely active, you may need to feed them more than the package suggests as well as offer healthy snacks like fruits and vegetable. Be sure to check in with your vet for advice on feeding your Bichon if he is highly active or training for an event to make sure his dietary needs are being met.

Senior dogs have lower calorie needs. Choose food designed for senior small dogs. Offer them 300-500 calories a day (including treats) and adjust the amounts incrementally to increase or reduce weight. Senior dogs will often begin to have a decreased appetite. This is not necessarily cause for alarm unless your pet refuses to eat at all, in which case you should consult a vet immediately. Continue to offer hard food, crunchy treats, or crispy fruits and vegetables as long as your senior dog is able to eat them, as it helps keep teeth healthy.

Easy Tips and Tricks to Control and Reduce Weight

- Read food packaging to determine the manufacturer's feeding guidelines.
- Measure the food with a measuring cup or scoop.
- Maintain a consistent feeding schedule so your dog doesn't overeat because he is worried about not being fed regularly.
- Keep your pet active. Consider hiring a dog walker if exercising your pet isn't possible on a regular basis.
- Offer healthy snacks like real jerky and sliced fruits and vegetables.
- Limit the number of treats each day.
- Avoid or severely limit rich food and fast foods.
- Don't give your dog bones and fats from meats; avoid gravies and excessively greasy foods and butter.
- Keep your dog out of the trash. Bichons can be very determined to get into trash bags and containers.

Homemade Food and Recipes

Many Bichon owners choose to make all or part of their dog's food at home. There are a variety of reasons why some people choose to be a chef to their pups. Some owners are disenchanted with the dog food industry, feeling that the companies don't have their dog's best interest at heart, fearing that the food could be unhealthy or dangerous to their dogs. Some owners just prefer to know exactly what their dogs are eating and feel better being able to control the freshness and quality of the ingredients, forgoing unknown or undesirable ingredients, fillers, or preservatives. But often pet owners choose homecooked meals for health reasons specific to their pets such as food allergies, diabetes, or weight management. Depending on

*Photo Courtesy of
Mary Roti*

your vet, they may even recommend a highly specific diet for your Bichon's health needs. Another reason is simply because they enjoy doing it. Cooking for our Bichons can be rewarding and enjoyable. And the best part is watching them enjoying a meal that we prepared with love!

When choosing food to make for your dog at home, remember that you will need to choose ingredients that are safe, and you should not switch a dog to all home-cooked meals without consulting your vet to determine if the food you have selected will contain the correct proportions of protein, fat, carbohydrates, vitamins, minerals, omega-3 fatty acids, fiber, and taurine. Your dog's allergies and sensitivities will have to be carefully monitored.

Ask your pet's doctor if they think that homemade food is an acceptable part of your Bichon's diet. I have made a decision to feed my pets 95% kibble and about 5% homemade for variety, and because I enjoy seeing my dogs get excited. But truth be told, my dogs are excited about their kibble every time and at ages three, five, and eleven, all of my dogs are fortunately in excellent health. There are debates among Bichon owners about everything from nutrition to wardrobe, and that's okay. Choose what is right for you and your budget and time, and for your pup.

Easy kibble or canned food "toppers"

- Frozen or fresh blueberries
- Diced apples
- Unsalted peas cooked, frozen, or fresh
- Chopped carrots (raw or cooked)
- Chickpeas or beans rinsed
- Green beans drained
- Crumbled cooked ground beef, turkey, or chicken
- Baked and cut up fish (like salmon or tilapia)
- Rice or couscous
- Scrambled eggs
- Bacon crumbles: When we overcook bacon, first we cry a little, then we like to let it cool and crumble it for salads, and then sprinkle a little bit on our dogs' kibble.
- Chia seeds, pumpkin seeds, or flaxseed
- Small amounts of olive oil or coconut oil
- Pureed plain pumpkin

Bland food for upset stomachs

Boil bone-in chicken breast and remove skin and bones from the pot, then remove the chicken and place it on a cutting board to cool. Using two forks (or your hands) tear the chicken into shreds. Mix with cooked white rice (which is easier to digest than brown rice).

Homemade Broth

For simple broth, retain the liquid from boiling the chicken and pour the broth through a strainer and separate into 8- or 16-ounce glass or plastic containers and refrigerate or freeze. Freeze broth that won't be used within five days and use all broth within five days of thawing.

I also like to use jumbo silicone ice cube trays to freeze small servings of broth that can easily be popped out and thawed for my dogs within 60 seconds in the microwave. Serve at room temp or warm, but not hot.

Baked Sweet Potato

Wash the sweet potato and leave the skin on. Pierce the skin 4-5 times with a fork and wrap in parchment paper and microwave it for 6-10 minutes (depending on size) until it is soft all the way through. Allow to cool to a safe temperature and slice into chunks or mash 2-3 tablespoons to add to the dog food. No seasoning is needed.

PUMPKIN PANCAKES RECIPE

- 1 cup plain pumpkin puree
- 1/4 cup milk of choice–oat milk or plant-based milk is my preference. Avoid nut milks because dogs cannot have tree nuts.
- 1 tablespoon coconut oil melted, or olive oil, or use a non-stick pan
- 2 eggs
- 1 cup oat flour (use old-fashioned oats and grind until you have a cup of flour)
- 1/2 teaspoon baking soda
- 1/8 teaspoon salt
- 1/8 teaspoon ground cinnamon
- 1 tsp of ground flaxseed or chia seeds (for fiber)

In a small bowl, whisk the eggs, then add the pumpkin and then the milk. In a separate medium bowl, mix the dry ingredients. Create a hole in the middle of the dry ingredients, then stir the wet ingredients into it.

Pour onto preheated skillet creating pancakes that are 3-4 inches in diameter.

Cook on low to medium low heat flipping after the edges become formed. Cook all the way through. Cool before serving.

CHAPTER 15
Grooming Your Bichon

Coat Basics

Bichon Frise translates to "Curly Lap Dog" in French, and Bichon lovers everywhere can agree that their curly hair and loving temperament are a wonderful combination. Bichons have hair instead of fur. They shed very little and are considered hypoallergenic (there is no completely hypoallergenic dog, but Bichons are easier on allergies than many other dogs). The only time my Bichon sheds is when I am actively combing or brushing him. Otherwise, I have never found even a piece of his hair on my clothes or furniture. I can't say the same for his muddy paw prints, however.

Photo Courtesy of Kim Cawley

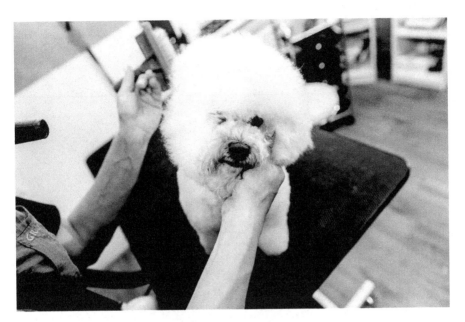

Brushing and Bathing

Brushing

Due to how curly the Bichon coat is, it can tangle and mat easily. This is why regular combing, brushing, and trimming is required. Fortunately, Bichons love being in their owners' laps, so if you can make it a positive experience for your dog, combing and brushing regularly should be relatively easy for both of you.

If your Bichon is matted, I highly recommend a professional cut. The groomer may suggest that your Bichon's hair be cut short. This is because splitting mats in their tight, curly hair can be very painful, and most groomers will recommend the most humane option. Unless you have a show dog, trimming your dog's hair temporarily might be the best bet. Don't worry. Bichons' hair grows and fills in rather quickly.

Regular Grooming

You should be prepared to groom your pup about twice a week. It shouldn't take more than 30 minutes and you can do it while you watch TV, listen to a podcast, or even sit outside under a tree.

Start grooming your Bichon when he is very young. Initially it won't take more than a few minutes but it's helpful to get him used to the tools you will be using throughout his life. This way, he won't run from you when he sees the comb or brush.

Photo Courtesy of
Sheryn Turner

Tools Needed

For daily brushing you will need:

- A metal dog comb
- A slicker brush
- A mat splitter
- Cornstarch powder
- Treats
- A small caddy for your supplies

The Basics

Create a relaxing environment for your pup. Have him lie down on a blanket or towel on your lap with all of your supplies close at hand. Start in an area of your pup's body that he enjoys having petted or groomed, preferably an area without tangles. Comb the direction of the hair growth, from the head toward the tail. If you find a tangled area, work around it at the start.

HELPFUL TIP
A Comb is Key

With their curly hair, Bichons need to be brushed several times a week to prevent mats from forming. One common problem that new Bichon owners run into, however, is that they tend to only brush the top layer of fur, while the hair closest to the skin becomes matted. You should be able to get a metal comb all the way down to your dog's skin, through every inch of fur—use a brush to remove tangles before they become mats.

Groom small sections at a time, offering your dog lots of gentle praise and an occasional treat. If his hair is hard to brush due to the length or tangles, add a little cornstarch to the tangled areas and work it in while you gently separate the tangled hair with your fingers. Once it is reasonably separated, you can work the slicker brush through it. If it is still tangled, try a spray detangler product.

If you can tell it is hurting your pup, take a break or work on a different section. It may take you a few days to brush him thoroughly if it has been a while. Be patient and don't force the process. This should be a bonding time, not torture.

Remember to brush every part of your pup. Don't forget the tail, inside the leg joints, behind the knees, under the neck, under the ear flaps and the face. I like to do the tail and face last, because my Bichon is not too fond of having these areas groomed. Grooming isn't his favorite activity, but he trusts me and he lets me do what is needed, as long as we don't find a painful mat.

Bathing

Bichons should be combed out and free of tangles and mats before they are bathed. Otherwise, their delicate and curly hair will tighten even

Photo Courtesy of
Katie Linacre

further, increasing your workload and the likelihood that you will need to take your dog to the groomer for professional assistance.

You can bathe your Bichon in your sink or shower, or you can take him to a local pet store that has a public dog bath that you can pay a small fee to use.

Supplies you will need for your dog's bath:

- Dog shampoo
- Conditioner
- Cotton balls
- Two towels
- A slip leash

Choosing Shampoo and Conditioner

A Bichon's bright white coat is one of its most noticeable traits. But keeping a Bichon white and clean is not always easy, especially with active outdoor personalities like my Bichon. He lives for a good run on our land and a satisfying roll in the dirt. He doesn't care how much time or money I spent making him look extra adorable and fluffy.

Fortunately, there are whitening shampoos for dogs. When you squeeze this kind of shampoo into your hand, it will be very purple. Don't panic. It will not turn your dog purple (unless you let it sit for quite a long time). I like to wash my dog twice (since he loves to get dirty) so I bathe him once with a gentle oatmeal shampoo, then rinse him completely and wash him again with the whitening shampoo.

You may also wish to get a conditioner for your Bichon to make combing out after the bath and blow dry a little easier. You can also combine vinegar and water and pour it over your dog after his bath, and then rinse him several times with cool water. This is good for the coat and skin.

Bathing Process & Safety

Never leave your dog in the bath, shower, tub, or sink unattended. Never leave him attached to a leash while you walk out of the room because dogs like to follow people and he could choke himself. Always test the water temperature before directing any water at your dog. Be prepared before you start the grooming process because once you start, you shouldn't leave your dog unattended.

Here are the basic steps:

STEP 1 Set up your bathing area with all of the needed supplies and begin to warm the water to the correct temperature so you don't startle your dog with cold water or burn him with hot water.

STEP 2 Remove your dog's collar and slide a slip leash around his neck so you can maintain control. If this step isn't needed, just skip it.

STEP 3 Put cotton balls in your dog's ears so he doesn't get ears full of water.

STEP 4 Wet your dog all over and apply shampoo, scrubbing his hair gently, remembering to get his tail and face. Be careful but thorough around the face, remembering to guard his eyes from shampoo and not to pour water into his nose. Allow the shampoo to sit a couple of minutes, but not long enough to dry out or irritate the skin.

STEP 5 Rinse your dog completely using warm water from a sprayer or a cup. Repeat shampooing if necessary, to remove all dirt.

STEP 6 For stained areas (usually muddy legs on my dog), combine hydrogen peroxide and cornstarch into a paste and then apply. Leave on 5-10 minutes and then rinse off.

STEP 7 Optional: use a conditioner or a vinegar and water rinse. Rinse completely with cool (not cold) water.

STEP 8 Since Bichons' hair can hold a lot of water, run your hands down your dog's body, squeezing out excess water as you go.

STEP 9 Wrap your dog up in a towel and press the towel into the hair to pull out more water, compressing the body, legs, tail, and face, then transfer your Bichon to a second towel to keep your pup warm. If you have a helper, you can get them to grab a warm towel from the dryer for this part.

STEP 10 Cuddle and praise your pet, and then get ready to blow dry!

Note: If your dog's bottom is matted and dirty with excrement, use a comb and a small pair of scissors (and gloves) to clean the area prior to bathing. Once trimmed, if you notice that the skin is red and irritated, use a cotton ball soaked in witch hazel to further clean and soothe the area.

Blow Drying

For this step you can use a regular hair dryer, a special dog dryer or a fan. I prefer something heated (but not too hot), so I don't use a fan. Plus, the idea of being in a crate while air blows on me sounds terrible, so I don't choose this option for Ricky. If you choose to fan dry your dog, remember not to turn the fan up too high and do not put it too close to the crate. You don't want to take your dog's breath away, so set the fan so it's indirectly pointed at the crate, not head on. Make sure that the room is warm enough that it doesn't feel like a chilly windstorm for your dog. Ricky prefers to stay wrapped up while I blow dry him in sections, but you don't have to do that.

While blow drying, use a slicker brush to simultaneously brush your dog's hair. Brush and dry one section at a time, taking care not to use too much heat. Hold the dryer away from your pet's skin and keep the dryer on a lower heat setting until you are comfortable with the process.

Here's a suggested order for blow drying:

1. Tail and bottom

2. Legs

3. Underside

4. Sides and back

5. Chest and neck

6. Face and ears (remember to remove the cotton balls)

Using this method, your Bichon will be soft and fluffy, and his curls will be indistinct and more cloudlike. It is okay to let your Bichon air-dry but remember to keep him out of the yard and the cold until he is fully dry. And also remember that the curls will be tighter and harder (but not impossible) to brush out later.

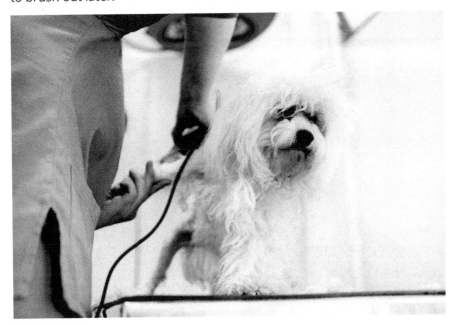

Trimming the Nails

If your dog's nails touch the floor when he is standing flat on his paws, then the nails are too long. Nails that are too long are more likely to get chipped, split, or accidentally caught on something, which can lead to a very painful injury.

Many people are intimidated by nail trimming because they are afraid to cut the nails too short and accidentally hurt their dogs. And if your dog has had a nail cut too short, he probably will be timid or frightened about getting his nails trimmed. But nail trimming doesn't have to be daunting for you or for your Bichon.

First choose your method of nail trimming. There are traditional nail trimmers for dogs as well as nail grinders. What you use depends on your comfort level and what you think will create the best experience for your dog. If you choose to use trimmers, get a quality pair that will cut the nails cleanly. The edges can still be sharp however, so plan to file the nails as well. Get some styptic powder in case you cut a nail too short and it bleeds.

The steps:

STEP 1 Sit comfortably with your dog. Stay relaxed. Ask for a hand if you don't want to do it alone but remember not to overwhelm your dog by making him feel trapped.

STEP 2 If using a grinder, trim the hair around the paws first so it doesn't get caught in the grinder. If using trimmers, you can skip this step. However, you might have an easier time seeing what you are doing if you do a little hair trimming first.

STEP 3 Take your time. You don't have to do it all at once. If you can only do a paw at a time, that's okay. Take breaks, offer treats, or even play a little.

STEP 4 Only cut off the white tips of the nails, being careful not to cut into the pink area. If you trim a nail too short, and it bleeds, simply dip it into the styptic powder and shake off the excess.

STEP 5 Remember to cut the nails on the dew claws as well.

STEP 6 File the nails with a metal file if needed.

If a nail is broken or damaged, it's wise to get the vet to take a look at it. A broken nail can be very painful for dogs and it can also get infected.

Pro tip

Start trimming your dog's nails when he is a puppy if possible. This will help him trust the process and add to your confidence early on.

Brushing Their Teeth

It's recommended that you brush your dog's teeth 2-3 times a week for good dental health and for fresher breath. Toothpaste and toothbrushes for your dog can easily be purchased online or at a pet store. Never use toothpaste for people, which contains ingredients that are toxic to dogs. You can also use gauze wrapped around your finger, or a washcloth. In lieu of dog toothpaste, you can make a paste with baking soda and water and apply it to the toothbrush.

Before going all out with the toothbrushing party, start by massaging your dog's gums. This allows him to get comfortable with you having your hand in his mouth. It may take time for your dog to get used to you providing dental care for him. Also let him taste the toothpaste in advance to make sure he's okay with it.

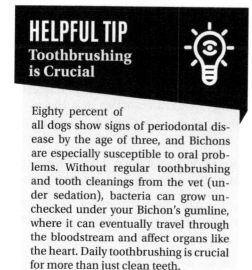

HELPFUL TIP
Toothbrushing is Crucial

Eighty percent of all dogs show signs of periodontal disease by the age of three, and Bichons are especially susceptible to oral problems. Without regular toothbrushing and tooth cleanings from the vet (under sedation), bacteria can grow unchecked under your Bichon's gumline, where it can eventually travel through the bloodstream and affect organs like the heart. Daily toothbrushing is crucial for more than just clean teeth.

When he's comfortable with having your fingers in his mouth, add a small amount of toothpaste to the brush and brush his teeth at a 45-degree angle in a circular motion. Start in the dirtiest areas first in case he becomes uncooperative early on. As with nail trimming, it may take more than one attempt before you reach your goal.

There are tooth cleaning toys that may interest your dog and keep his teeth relatively clean between brushings. You should also talk to your vet about taking your Bichon for a professional dental cleaning once a year.

Look for hard snacks and treats that are designed to help remove plaque and consider a water additive designed for dogs that can help with bad breath and gentle plaque removal.

Cleaning Ears, Eyes, and Mouth

"You may notice your Bichon getting eye stains and goop in their tear ducts. We call them eye boogers! This is normal and new owners must wash their face regularly."

Vicki Turner
Turner Dog Ranch

The clothes might make the man, but the face makes the pup. Let's face it, Bichons have utterly adorable faces, and we want them to look their best! That means clean and fresh smelling ears, clean eyes without tears stains, and a cute little mouth and muzzle that doesn't look stained.

Ears

Ears are pretty easy to clean! You can purchase a commercial ear cleaner to mix one part vinegar or peroxide with two parts warm water. Squeeze

a little into each ear and massage into the ears by squeezing and massaging the ear flaps against the ear canals. Be prepared: your dog will definitely shake his head to get the water out. This is part of the process. Once your pup gives his head a couple of good shakes, wipe out the inside of his ears with a couple of jumbo cotton balls. Never use cotton swabs inside your dog's ears because they can force dirt and debris deeper into his ears which can lead to infection or can cause damage to the inner ear.

Eyes

One of the questions I am asked the most about Bichons is about their pink, red, or brown tear stains. Since they truly are stains, they are not easy to remove. But tear stains can be greatly improved, and with a bit of luck and diligence, eliminated.

Tear stains are a result of runny eyes, which can occur for many reasons. Wiping your Bichon's eyes and the area around his eyes daily will help keep the stains from building up. You can also use an eyebrow comb, dis-

167

posable mascara wand, a clean toothbrush, or a small fine-tooth comb to brush the "goop" out of his eyes. Make sure your pup is calm while you do this. You may have to grasp his snout very gently to hold him steady, so you don't poke him in the eye.

You can also use a couple of cotton swabs dipped in peroxide to gently wipe the area clean. Be careful not to get it in your dog's eyes. Lastly, you can get a small pair of scissors and trim any stained hair that is long enough to cut. But if you are not confident that your Bichon will stay still while you do this, leave this work to the groomer.

There are products that are designed to help with tear stains, but the reviews are mixed. The cleaning products can be pricey and may not work better than an inexpensive bottle of peroxide and some cotton balls or cotton swabs. There are also commercial eye cleaning pads, or you can get eye wash from your vet to help rinse your dog's eyes and clean the area around them. Additionally, many Bichon owners opt to give their dogs distilled water only, as it is reported to help prevent tear stains, by containing fewer minerals than tap water. Another tip for prevention is to add a tiny bit of apple cider vinegar to your dog's drinking water and add a probiotic supplement to his diet.

Getting rid of tear stains can be a two steps forward, one step back process, and it might be something you battle perpetually. Some of you will get lucky and get a Bichon that doesn't get troublesome staining, or you might find the perfect combination that works for your dog. In my experience, results are cumulative, so it might take time, a variety of methods, and patience to reach your desired result.

Mouth and Beard

After shampooing and drying your Bichon, you might still see some brown or rust color staining on the mouth area. This is where a pair of thinning scissors come in handy. Using a conservative approach, trim a little of the stained area and then check your progress. Trim a little more until you get the worst of the staining thinned out. Then you can use hydrogen peroxide and apply it to the mouth area and let it sit for several minutes. You will see the color fade quite a bit.

When Professional Help Is Necessary

"I recommend you get your Bichon professionally groomed at least every ten weeks in addition to brushing or combing on a daily basis, or else their coats will mat."

Jeanette Neagu
Takoda Dogs

If you are like many Bichon owners, you will choose a hybrid of professional care and home care. There may be times when you feel like you need to get help with grooming or maybe you will just prefer it. Here are times to consider taking your Bichon to a groomer.

Tangles and mats – As previously discussed, tangles and mats can be a big challenge. If your Bichon becomes too matted for you to brush or clip his hair without causing him discomfort, make an appointment for the groomer.

Hot spots – If your dog is missing patches of hair, you should take him to the vet so they can determine the cause and a source of treatment. Don't allow the spots to become raw and painful.

Nails – If trimming your dog's nails is a stressful ordeal, ask your vet to do it when you are there for an exam or a visit. If your dog is professionally groomed, this usually includes a nail trim. You can also schedule a nail trim only with your vet or groomer.

Photo Time – If you have family photos or a special occasion on the horizon, plan ahead and schedule a grooming appointment in advance. Holidays are very busy times for groomers and they can be booked out months in advance.

Tips for Working with the Groomer

I have seen a lot of complaints and bad reviews about groomers. Some of them are related to safety, but others are related to bad haircuts and unmet expectations. Here are some tips for maintaining a good working relationship with your dog's groomer:

- **Bring sample photos** – There are different terms for different cuts so find a photo that shows the haircut you would like for your Bichon.
- **Have realistic expectations** – If you want your Bichon to have a fluffy white show dog cut and style, but your Bichon is heavily matted, you might be barking up the wrong tree. A dog with mats may need a very short cut to start over. Groomers are not magicians. They can only work with what they are given.

- **Meet the groomer** – If you are trying out a new groomer, call ahead to see if you can meet with them face to face when you arrive so you can review your expectations and goals directly.

- **Tip** – Tipping is not required but it is definitely appreciated and is also a great way to help your groomer remember you fondly.

- **Be honest** – When you return to your groomer for the next cut, tell them if there is anything you would like to do differently than last time. Most groomers will appreciate the feedback and direction. If they don't, then you might consider changing groomers.

- **Do your part** – If you have dreams of a puffy and fluffy Bichon bouncing around, be prepared to put a lot of work into grooming at home. You will need to do daily brushing to keep your Bichon looking so good, and you are going to have to work hard to keep your energetic dog from bouncing into puddles.

Choose a haircut that fits your lifestyle –

- A **show cut** is very fluffy, full, and round; it is so round that your dog's ears may appear as if they just blend into the round puffy head. It requires the most effort and expense to keep it up. This is not a realistic year-round goal for most Bichon owners but it might be an occasional goal when you really want your Bichon to stand out.

- A **puppy cut** (also known as a lamb cut) is a medium length body cut with a round face that has enough length to appear rounded without having the curls brushed into a dome. The tail also keeps some length.

- The **utility cut** is a short cut all over that will take away a lot of the round "teddy bear" look. This is a great option for a Bichon that is outdoorsy and loves to get dirty. It requires less brushing, and if regularly cut, it prevents mats almost entirely. That said, you will still need to brush your dog's tail and ears regularly to prevent matting.

There are other styles to choose from, so look at photos and talk to your groomer about what fits your lifestyle, your dog's preferences, and his personality the best.

CHAPTER 16
Basic Health Care

Visiting the Vet

Going to the vet can be very stressful for many pets, but it can and should be a positive experience. While your dog may not do back flips over getting shots, he should be relatively calm and trusting if you have trained him right. Here are some tips to help make vet visits as positive as possible:

- Groom and handle your Bichon regularly and with calming confidence. Help him get used to being handled by touching his paw pads, washing between his toes, cleaning his ears, brushing his teeth, clipping his nails, wiping around his eyes, etc. Also hold your pup in a cradle position (on his back) in your arms. This may take some getting used to. Try distracting him with a treat or a bit of peanut butter to help him get used to being rolled over.

- Get your Bichon used to the crate. Make the crate a special and re-warding place by offering special treats and toys when he is in the crate. Offer praise and a soothing voice.

- Make car rides fun. As discussed in the chapter about travel, many Bichons will love car travel right away while others will take more time to adjust to it. It is important not to only take them in the car when they are going to the vet. I like to randomly take my dogs with me when I can just so they stay excited about being in the car.

- Visit the vet in advance. Before your dog needs to be vaccinated or handled by the vet and vet techs, take him in for a friendly visit. A friendly visit should be scheduled in advance and is a chance for your pet to sniff, meet, cuddle, play and get treats. If possible, do this more than once.

- When it's time to go to the vet, stay calm! You can't get amped up and expect your Bichon to stay relaxed. He is very sensitive to your moods and emotions. If you get anxious about taking your pet to the vet, then you need to work on yourself first. Adjust your mood before interacting with your pet. If you can't remain calm, ask your partner or a friend to come with you to be supportive to you so you can then be supportive for your dog.

- Do not assume your dog is anxious even if you are. You could easily upset a pet that was good to go before your emotions negatively im-pacted him.

- A sedative-free, unmuzzled visit is ideal. To help create a low-stress visit, ask your vet for appointments when the clinic isn't at its busi-est. If your pet is anxious or has had bad experiences at the vet, call ahead to ask if they can have an exam room ready for you so you don't have to sit in the waiting room with a trembling pup. Also, cre-ate some personal space for your dog and let other customers know if your pet is scared and will not enjoy being petted. Do not allow oth-er animals to greet your dog if your dog is not comfortable with that. Speak softly to your pet and pull his face toward you if something or someone seems to unsettle him.

Creating a calm experience for the pet is the pet owner's responsibility. However, that doesn't mean that you will have full control over everything that occurs or how your Bichon feels. If your Bichon came to you from an-other family or a shelter, or has had unsettling experiences with the vet, or with people in general, you may see moderate to severe anxiety in your Bi-chon. If this is the case, make an appointment to speak with the vet before taking your dog for an exam or medical care. This will allow you the opportunity to discuss options to calm your pet that may include an anxiety medication. While this may not be your preference, remember that exams and vaccines are essential and unavoidable, so you must have a plan. Lastly, remember to not expect perfection from yourself or from your dog. Plan, prepare, smile, breathe, and stay calm. You've got this.

Fleas and Ticks

I don't know about you, but just the idea of fleas or ticks makes my skin crawl. When we first moved to the country, we had no idea how serious the tick problem could be. Needless to say, we found out the hard way when we found ticks on ourselves and the dogs. And the dogs were already on year-round flea and tick protection. We jokingly call these ticks "country strong" because they take a licking and keep on ticking. But seriously, fleas and ticks are not only annoying, they can be very dangerous to you or your pets. Don't mistake their tiny size as being a small problem.

Photo Courtesy of
Courtney Noelting

Fleas

Flea bites are very itchy to humans and animals and can cause an allergic reaction in either. And once they make themselves comfortable in your home, they can be quite difficult and expensive to get rid of them. It's best to do everything possible to avoid this problem to begin with.

Fleas can transmit parasites like tapeworms to your pets and can cause dermatitis that may cause your pet to chew or scratch his skin, which can be painful and even become infected causing costly vet bills to treat.

Ticks

Ticks are very uncomfortable to deal with and can be very dangerous to humans and animals, as they transmit several diseases. The most common disease spread to humans and dogs is Lyme disease, which is typically characterized by fever, rash, and achiness.

Whenever you and your dogs are outside, especially on trails and in wooded areas, it is vital that you check your pets for ticks. If you can remove ticks early, especially before they latch onto the skin, you greatly reduce the risk of illness. You might be surprised at how crafty ticks are at hiding on your dog's body. Check your dog's groin, around the hip joints, under the collar, and even in his ears.

Prevention

There are several different flea and tick prevention options; some over the counter, some from your vet, and others can be made at home.

For simple prevention, use insect repellant or a natural alternative like an essential oil blend for repelling insects. With natural options, be prepared to reapply often and to carry the product with you on your walk or time outside.

There are flea and tick collars that you can place on your dog to repel insects. When choosing one, do your research and learn about potential side effects that could occur. Also, make sure to mark on your calendar to remind you when to replace the collar. A reputable collar can last 6-8 months. Less expensive collars last just 4-8 weeks. Also, make sure to check the minimum age for the use of the collar on your dog.

Topical monthly flea prevention is relatively affordable and is easy to use. Typically, the liquid just needs to be applied between the shoulder blades once a month for full coverage. In areas experiencing a bad flea and tick problem, you may have to supplement the topical usage with a collar or an oral option. You will also have to prevent your dog's fur from getting wet for the first 24 hours after the product has been applied. You may have to separate your dogs if one of them likes to lick the medicine off of his brother or sister's coat.

There are risks to consider when using topical treatments and collars. These forms of flea prevention have been shown to cause major health problems including severe dermatitis, seizure and even death in animals. Flea collars and topical solutions can also pose a risk to small children and pregnant women, and the chemicals used could pose a risk for weeks after the collar has been removed. Additionally, young puppies, pregnant dogs, nursing dogs or senior dogs should not use flea collars or topical flea prevention as the health risks are even more severe for them and their offspring. You should read the pamphlet information and warnings for all flea products including those that claim to be "natural" as this in no way guarantees safety.

Oral flea and tick prevention is extremely convenient. The active ingredient is combined with a flavored treat to easily administer to your pet. Unfortunately, not all dogs will like the taste, so be prepared to add it to something tasty or even grind it up into a poultice to add it to his food or something moist. Using oral flea and tick prevention is easy because you don't have to worry about a lost or damaged collar or a wet topical medicine soaking into the fur before something goes wrong. You just have to make sure that your dog actually eats the entire pill and you may have to separate multiple pets to ensure that each one only eats his own tablet. Please read all information and warnings for oral flea and tick prevention before administering to your Bichon and always follow the recommended doses carefully.

For less intrusive flea and tick treatment, regularly vacuum your home and furniture, bathe and comb your pets (with a flea comb), and wash their bedding regularly. Do not allow pets with fleas into your bed. Promptly remove fleas and ticks from your pets.

Treating Puppies

The minimum age and weight requirements vary for different flea and tick products. Do not attempt to use any products on your puppy until they meet the recommended age and weight. In the meantime, if you find fleas on your puppy, wash him with warm water and use a flea comb to remove any fleas. Be sure to kill the fleas to be certain that they will not just relocate themselves. Do not use flea shampoos on small puppies and always choose shampoos that are gentle and non-drying. Dilute the shampoo, or skip shampoo altogether, and just rinse your puppy well with warm water.

The Bottom Line

It might be tempting to forgo flea and tick prevention, but it's important to know the risks in your area and to respond and prepare appropriately. Educate yourself on the types of ticks and diseases spread by ticks and watch for those symptoms in your Bichon and in yourself and family. And remember, fleas and ticks can survive winter, meaning there is no safe time to ignore the need to prevent fleas and ticks in your family and household.

Worms and Parasites

Worms and parasites exist in all 50 states, during all seasons, regardless of the weather. Thus, the treatment and prevention of worms and parasites should be a primary priority for all dog owners.

Worms are a real concern for all dog owners. About one in three dogs will test positive for worms at one point in their lives. As is true with fleas and ticks, preventing worms is the best course of action to prevent harmful worms from causing illness, or death, in your Bichon.

There are several types of worms that dogs can get such as heartworm, tapeworms, hookworms, roundworms and whipworms. All of these, except heartworms, are intestinal parasites. Some, like tapeworms, are usually easy to spot because they are easily visible in their fecal matter (often described as looking like pieces of rice). Intestinal parasites are worms that live in the intestines and feed off the food the dog consumes, or off of the dog's cellular matter. Hookworms are unique because they actually hook themselves to the lining of the intestinal wall and live off of the blood vessels of the lining, which can potentially lead to anemia.

These parasites can lead to discomfort and a myriad of health problems and symptoms. Common symptoms of worms may include diarrhea, vomiting, lethargy, distended belly, loss of or increased appetite, weight changes, rashes, dry skin or dull coat, itchy skin, or dogs scooting their bottoms along the floor. All of these symptoms are considered potentially serious, and you should seek medical advice and treatment quickly. These symptoms could also be indicators of many other illnesses, so always take note when you see your dog behaving or appearing differently than normal and contact your vet.

Heartworm disease, on the other hand, is not so obvious because the first noticeable symptom is usually coughing in your dog. Heartworm disease takes about seven months to develop after a dog is bitten by an infected mosquito because the larvae has to develop through the life cycle to become active adult worms. About one in two hundred dogs will get heartworm each year. To prevent heartworms, keep your dog on heartworm prevention year-round. Set a notification on your phone or mark your calendar for the same day each month so you can provide the medicine consistently. Many dog owners give their dogs their monthly meds on the first of each month, but I suggest you choose a day that is easy for you to remember.

Additionally, keep your yard clean and pick up the fecal matter often. Do not allow your pup to eat the waste and wash your hands after cleaning up potty messes in the yard and the house. Keep fleas off your dog by using reputable flea prevention and treating fleas in your home quickly and aggressively. Deworming medicine is available at pet stores, online, and at farm supply stores. Deworming medication is a liquid oral medication that is easy to give to your pup by measuring the correct amount of medication into an oral syringe and squeezing it into the back of his mouth. Follow your vet's recommended deworming schedule for your puppy or follow the instructions on the deworming package. Have your vet check your dog's waste for worms annually and react promptly to symptoms of worms.

Ringworm

Ringworm is not actually a worm at all; it is a fungus which is passed through spores. But due to its misleading name, many people often assume that it's a worm. Ringworm is contagious to humans, dogs, and other animals so it can be passed from you to your dog, your dog to you, between people, or between dogs. Ringworm usually looks like a reddish ring on the skin with a hollow center, or it may be gray and scaly. A "crust" may or may not be present. In dogs, it may cause patchy hair loss. If you believe that your dog has ringworm, your vet can examine your dog, or may even do testing. Ringworm can be treated with oral medication and with topical creams and specialty shampoos.

Other Parasites

Giardia and cryptosporidium are parasites that live in the intestinal tract of dogs. Both are contracted when dogs consume food, soil, or water contaminated by fecal matter. Giardia is characterized by diarrhea, vomiting, and dehydration. Cryptosporidium is characterized by fever, diarrhea, lethargy, and loss of appetite.

To prevent giardia and cryptosporidium, do not allow your dog to drink from puddles, standing water, or other outdoor sources, even those that appear to be clean. Giardia and cryptosporidium are both microscopic protozoan parasites that you cannot see or smell. They can be spread to humans and animals, so it's essential to carry enough water for you and your dog when you go on hikes, picnics, and other outdoor adventures. Another option is to purchase a portable microfilter to filter any outdoor water before offering it to your dog to drink. While camping, you can also bring the water to a full boil for a minimum of one minute and then allow to cool before drinking. Store the water in a cool location after treating it.

If you suspect that you or your dogs have contracted giardia, see your doctor or vet immediately. Common treatments are medication, IV fluids, and allowing the digestive tract to rest from food while it recovers. Easing back onto bland food that is easy to digest will benefit those infected. A follow-up appointment will generally be needed to make sure that reinfection has not occurred. Meanwhile, you will need to keep your dog and his surroundings clean and sanitized.

Holistic Alternatives and Supplements

In an effort to find more natural, less invasive, and less expensive options, many dog owners are seeking holistic alternatives to treating their dogs' health concerns. Whether you choose holistic, traditional, or complementary care, you are your dog's spokesperson and it's important to be informed and attentive and to communicate clearly with your dog's healthcare providers. Don't shy away from sharing with the vet that you have tried home remedies. While a vet may not share every viewpoint you have on home care, they should respect you as a pet owner.

A few holistic disciplines you might choose to consider are chiropractic care, massage therapy, aromatherapy, and sound therapy. There is a growing trend in veterinary medicine toward a more holistic approach and many vets are seeking continued education to reflect that trend. As people spend more money on themselves and family members on alternative medicine, they are also becoming increasingly interested in helping their pets live long and healthy lives in the most natural way possible.

Chiropractic Care, Massage Therapy & Acupuncture

Chiropractic care for dogs is typically used to treat joint, muscle, and spine problems, but can also be useful in the treatment of urinary incontinence, hip dysplasia, injury, and recovery from surgery. When looking for a canine chiropractor you have two primary options: a veterinarian with an extensive background, education, and certification in veterinary chiropractic medicine, or you can choose a chiropractic doctor who has a strong background, education, and certification in animal chiropractic. Depending on your area, you may have to travel a bit to find a specialist in chiropractic care. Some of the reported benefits of chiropractic care are decreased pain, increased activity level and mobility, increased recovery time from surgeries or injuries, and increased quality of life. Chiropractic medicine could be a wonderful complementary practice to improve your pup's health and quality of life.

Massage Therapy is soothing and therapeutic manipulation of the muscles to encourage relaxation, decreased anxiety, improved circulation, decreased soreness, increased mobility, and improved sleep. A licensed massage therapist is typically qualified to perform massages on your dog; however, you should request information regarding their training, education, and potential certifications in canine massage. Massage therapy is more than just kneading and pressing on the muscles. It is a discipline that requires specialized training and experience in order to achieve specialized goals, especially in the arena of sports massage therapy and repetitive use recovery and therapy. However, if your primary goal is to help your dog relax, a massage at home will typically do the trick.

Here are some tips for giving your dog a massage:

- Choose a location that is easy on your body. I like to have my Bichon lie on my lap and then I rotate him as needed. You can choose to sit or stand.

- Avoid your dog's spine. You can run your fingers to either side of the spine, massaging the muscles parallel to it. Applying pressure directly on the spine can be painful and dangerous.

- Pay attention to your dog's reaction and adjust pressure accordingly. Maintain light but firm pressure and consider using slightly deeper pressure once the muscle group is warmed up. I know I am applying the right pressure when my pup's eyes start to close, and he looks deeply relaxed.

- Roll with it. Skin rolling is a great and simple technique, even for beginners, that increases circulation and is very relaxing to most dogs. Simply hold a section of skin between both hands and use your thumbs and forefingers to roll the skin gently in one continuous direction and then repeat. Prepare for drool.

Acupuncture is based on an Eastern philosophy of alternative or holistic medicine that uses tiny needles to treat pain and various ailments. While veterinarians around the country are offering acupuncture, it is still an unfamiliar resource for many pet owners. But for veterinary practices who have included acupuncture as a treatment option, there are many success stories both for the medical practice and for the animals who seem to be ben-efitting from the treatment.

In dogs, acupuncture is often used to decrease pain and increase range of motion for dogs with diseases or disorders that are from joint inflam-mation, degeneration, or injury. This is because the process helps to re-lease anti-inflammation and pain-relieving hormones. Acupuncture may also help dogs with allergies or dermatitis by increasing circulation to the inflamed areas which increase healing and decrease itching. Your vet may even suggest trying adding acupuncture to your dog's treatment regimen, while treating cancer with chemotherapy, to increase comfort and appetite.

Some pet owners opt to try acupuncture as a frontline approach be-fore trying pharmaceutical medications or surgeries. Other pet owners may choose to combine traditional Western medical options alongside acupunc-ture for a more holistic approach. Other pet owners may only consider acu-puncture as a last resort after all other options have been tried and failed (or success has been limited) or when the pet cannot tolerate tradition-al medications.

If you choose to try acupuncture for your pet, you should schedule a consultation with a licensed veterinarian with certification in acupuncture. They should be able to evaluate your dog's needs, answer all of your ques-tions, and assure you that the insertion of the small acupuncture needles should involve minimal to no pain and that once placed, should not hurt your dog at all.

Aromatherapy & Sound Therapy

Aromatherapy is the use of essential oils to affect the olfactory system of your dog to achieve a specific goal. Dogs can detect smells up to 100,000 times better than humans, making aromatherapy a natural and affordable option for treating issues like anxiety, skin irritation, upset stomachs, etc.

Here are some single ingredient options for use on or near your pet. There are also many blends for sale for specific uses.

- **Calming** | Lavender – Use lavender diluted in a glass spray bottle combined with water (shake well) and spritz your dog's coat or their bed or mix 1-2 drops with a carrier oil like coconut oil or olive oil and rub it on the ends of their ears. When traveling, try adding a couple of drops on a tissue and putting the tissue inside your car's air vent to help prevent motion sickness and anxiety.

- **Skin Irritations** | Roman Chamomile – Use Roman Chamomile in a carrier oil directly on the skin for anti-inflammatory and anti-parasitic benefits. It can also be combined with lavender for greater skin benefits.

- **Upset Stomach** | Ginger – Ginger is beneficial for decreasing nausea in dogs and people. For use on your Bichon, mix one to two drops with coconut oil and apply to your dog's paw so he can lick it off, or gently massage a few drops with a carrier oil into his stomach area.

- **Repelling Insects** | Lemongrass – Besides having a very fresh aroma, lemongrass is great at repelling fleas and mosquitos, and when mixed with lavender is also beneficial at repelling ticks. And if you or your pets are suffering from insect bites already, try mixing a few drops into your favorite oil to soothe you or your dog's itchy skin. A note of caution: essential oils are generally not as effective at repelling insects as products from the vet. Carefully weigh the benefits of using a natural option versus the risk of your dog becoming infected by a disease carried by fleas, ticks, or mosquitos. And as always, speak with your vet about all the ingredients that you use topically or internally for your pet.

There are many oils that are safe if used properly and responsibly. Similarly, there are many that are not safe for dogs at all. Be mindful to check the ingredients of any blended oils you buy before using them on your pets or diffusing them around your pets. And remember that a little goes a long way so use the oil in moderation, so you do not overwhelm your dog's senses.

While one bottle of a basic essential oil like lavender is generally affordable, buying several different kinds can get very pricey. Only buy what you can use within a year or two and make sure to store it in a cool area out of direct light. When making spray bottles of repellant or bedding spray, use a dark glass bottle to help it last longer. Store oils away from your pet's reach and always watch your dog for any unusual symptoms like itching, sneezing, drooling, lethargy, vomiting, or even seizures.

Sound therapy is the use of music, "white" noise, or other sound devices to soothe or calm your dogs. It's been a common practice for decades to leave on a radio or television for our pets. And there are many anecdotal stories about dogs reacting to animal sounds on TV or even dancing to their favorite songs.

As I sit with my three dogs writing, we are listening to music designed to calm dogs. What's special about it? The first layer of the song is a steady white noise; in this case, the white noise is rainfall. The white noise is then layered with the sound of birds lightly chirping. It is less steady, but the tone is consistent. The top note of the music consists of delicate bells chiming with a soft reverberation from the bells. My dogs are definitely relaxed. One of them began snoring about one minute into the song.

Sound therapy can be used to calm your dog while you are away, or while he is separate from you for any reason. Boarding facilities often install TVs in each room or put speakers throughout the boarding facility to offer a calming consistent sound to soothe the dogs. Many facilities swear by classical music, observing that the dogs sleep longer when it plays. I have found that nature sounds and lullabies are a huge hit with my dogs and the dogs I care for professionally. Another option I have found to be very useful is talk radio. The dogs don't care what the show hosts are talking about but hearing people calmly talk is reassuring for them. We use public radio and sports talk radio frequently.

If riding in the car or crate training brings up any anxiety for your pup, create a soothing sound environment for them. Layering sounds can be very calming. Buy a basic white noise machine, turn on a fan, or play music. Or do all three! During thunderstorms or fireworks, we turn the central heating and air fan to ON instead of AUTO and put multiple fans around the building. We then turn on calming music and diffuse lavender. Often the dog owners will contact me the next day to see how their dogs fared overnight, only to be surprised that their pups slept just fine. We can't control the world around us, but we can create a calming buffer that helps our dogs feel safe and secure.

Supplements

We love our pets like family so we want them to live a long and comfortable life. Every dog has different needs and not all issues will be met with basic nutrition. Dogs, like humans, all have individual needs and may need a little boost in certain areas. Here are some of the main areas of focus for the most commonly used supplements on the market.

Mobility
- Fish oil
- Glucosamine
- Chondroitin
- Methyl-sulfonyl-methane (typically referred to as MSM)

Skin & Allergies
- Coconut oil or medium chain triglycerides (nourishing to skin and coat)
- Omega 6 and 9 fatty acids (skin and coat)

- Fish oil – Salmon oil is an excellent source. This oil can be purchased in a liquid that can be pumped directly onto a dog's food.

- Turmeric (anti-inflammatory)

- Apple cider vinegar (helps dogs absorb vitamins and minerals from their food)

- Probiotics (helps with treatment of skin allergies)

Gastrointestinal

- From pre and Probiotics in capsules, to chewables or powders, these can be added to a dog's food to promote gut health by introducing healthy bacteria to the gut and digestive system.

- Yogurt (plain, no sweeteners, added to your dog's food in small quantities)

Calming & Anxiety Reducing

- Chamomile (relaxing)

- L-tryptophan (helps release serotonin)

- Valerian roots (calms hyperactivity)

- CBD Oil (hemp seed oil) NOTE: Hemp seed or CBD oil does not contain THC unless it is listed on the package. Look for terms like "full spectrum" to indicate that the product may contain a very small amount of THC that is considered beneficial in making the CBD effective for calming your pet and easing physical discomfort.

Aging

Senior vitamins containing:

- Co-Q10 (for heart health)

- Cod liver oil (for bones, teeth, skin, and coat)

- B vitamins (for energy)

- Vitamins A, C and E (for immunity)

Senior vitamins are generally recommended about 75-80% into a breed's average life expectancy or when a dog begins to show early signs of aging.

Final Thoughts

Mobility is a primary concern for most pet owners. And even though Bichons are a small breed, they can still face issues with their hips and joints. Hip dysplasia is a genetic deformity that can occur in Bichons and that can lead to arthritis. They can also suffer from luxating patellas where their knees get locked out of place or spinal arthritis. It's estimated that 80% or more of senior dogs experience joint inflammation or pain. To keep joints their healthiest, keep your Bichon at a healthy weight and give him plenty of exercise.

Bichons also are notorious for skin problems and sensitive stomachs, and often the two go hand in hand. For this reason, probiotic supplements or chewable over the counter "treats" with skin and digestion friendly ingredients are usually not only useful but essential for a dog's health. My Bichon was having regular skin issues that led him to self-groom excessively and chew on his paws and hindquarters until we added a daily probiotic supplement to his diet. He was initially not fond of eating them but once I started giving them to his siblings as well, he became very interested!

Follow the package and product instructions for dosages with any supplements and always discuss your intentions to add supplements with your vet. Pay attention to the fillers, flavors, proteins, and other ingredients listed to ensure that your pet does not have allergies or sensitivities to anything listed.

Vaccinations

Rabies

A rabies vaccine is required for all domestic animals for the safety of the pet, other animals, and humans. The vaccine is required at 3-4 months, with an annual booster or a 3-year vaccine (depending on the vaccine and the state requirements). Each state has different laws that dictate who may give the vaccine (such as a rabies officer, licensed veterinarian, vet tech, etc.), when the vaccine must first be administered, at what intervals boosters will be required, and what exemptions will be allowed (if any). If you have a pet that has had an allergic reaction to a rabies vaccine, discuss with your vet what to do to meet the requirements for an official exemption in your state.

When your dog is vaccinated, retain the original rabies certificate and attach the rabies tag to his collar securely. Do not let your pup out of the house without proper identification.

For state by state requirements, visit:

https://www.avma.org/sites/default/files/resources/Rabies-state-law-chart.pdf

DHPP

DHPP may also be called DA2PP or DAPP and includes Distemper, Hepatitis, Parainfluenza, and Parvovirus vaccines. It may also contain the Lep-

Photo Courtesy of
Mary Roti

tospirosis vaccine if recommended by your vet. This vaccine is also offered on a one or three year schedule depending on where you live and what your vet offers.

Bordetella

The Bordetella vaccine is used to prevent kennel cough and should be administered to dogs that will be kenneled or around other dogs

Kennel cough is highly contagious but can typically be prevented through vaccination which can be administered via injection or intranasal spray once or twice a year, based on the requirements of your vet clinic. The Bordetella nasal compound can also be purchased at farm supply stores, but your vet or boarding facility may require that all vaccines are provided by a licensed vet and therefore may require you to have this readministered by a vet before they can be kenneled, even for a one-day procedure or visit.

Leptospirosis

The "lepto" vaccine is not a required vaccine and is considered a "non-core" vaccine. I am choosing to include this vaccine in this chapter because some dogs are more susceptible to getting the virus and since the mortality rate for unvaccinated dogs with the virus is 25%, it's worthy of discussion.

The Leptospirosis virus is typically spread through dogs drinking stagnant water from puddles which has been contaminated by animal urine. Fall is a prominent season for the virus to spread and puppies and younger dogs are more susceptible to getting it. Talk to your vet to determine if your dog should get the leptospirosis vaccine and never let your dog drink stagnant water or melted snow.

Pet Insurance

With the advancements in medicine and medical care for animals, our pets are living longer than ever. But with a long life comes an increased cost of care. Naturally, it's worth the payoff!

Pet insurance is similar to medical insurance for humans. There are monthly premiums, deductibles, co-pays, and limitations to coverage. Choosing pet insurance requires research, budgeting, and long-term considerations.

Pricing for insurance depends primarily on the following factors:

- Age of the pet – The younger your dog is when you purchase the policy, the lower the premium. If you have more than one pet, you can choose which pets to cover

- What deductible you choose (a zero deductible being the most expensive)

- The amount of the copay (if there is a copay)

- The type of policy – Does it cover routine care and vaccines or just unexpected medical care? Does it cover pre-existing conditions? Does it cover hereditary issues that come up after the policy is in place?

- The fine print – Will the insurance still pay out if the pet dies during treatment? What procedures are excluded from the policy? Are all veterinary clinics "in network" or do they have a list of clinics that they cover? Are the payments from the insurance company to you capped and is there an annual or lifetime policy limit that restricts how much care the insurance company will cover?

- Does it cover prescription medications?

Also consider:
- Can you afford the monthly premium?

- Can you cover the deductible (your out-of-pocket expense per visit)? If you choose a $1,000 deductible to save on the cost of your monthly premium, but you can't afford the $1,000 out of pocket expense when needed, your insurance isn't going to be useful because you won't be able to afford to use it.

- Can you afford emergency care for your pet? If you can't afford a very large bill, but you can manage to cover a deductible, then insurance can be a life saver (literally and figuratively). This is typically referred to as catastrophic coverage because you are carrying a low cost/high deductible insurance in the event that something happens that is on a larger scale that you would not be able to cover on your own. In this coverage, you would pay for routine care on your own.

- Do you want routine care coverage (exams, vaccines, routine blood work, and dental cleanings) or just "accident and illness" coverage?

I chose a policy with a medium deductible that I can afford, but that also keeps my monthly *premium* affordable. I opted not to cover one of my pets, who was well into her years when I purchased the plan because the premium for her as a senior dog was too expensive. She is a healthy dog that has yet to require expensive medical care. I felt it made more financial sense to pay out of pocket for all of her accident and illness care since she is a ten-year-old boxer and has been sick only once in her life. I did choose to cover my four-year-old Labrador mix and my young Bichon. I am hoping that they will all live a very long time and I want to be prepared for anything! However, I chose to forgo the optional routine care coverage that I could have added on to the policy because I reviewed the cost of this care for my dogs over the last three years and the premium for the routine care coverage was about the same or a little more than just paying for the care out of pocket.

One last note: I recommend reviewing the process for submitting claims and finding out how long it will take to get reimbursed. Most pet insurance policies require you to pay the vet bills up front and then they will reimburse you after they receive a copy of all of the bills. Unless your vet will wait on payment from your insurance (most won't), then you will need to know who will actually be required to pay the bills on the front end, and if it's you, how long you will have to wait to be reimbursed by the insurance company. You may also be able to apply for credit that will cover most of your expenses until the insurance company cuts a check. You can ask your vet for credit options that the clinic accepts.

CHAPTER 17
Advanced Bichon Frise Health and Aging Dog Care

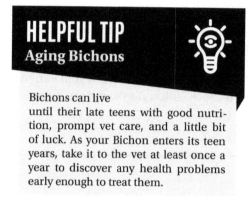

HELPFUL TIP
Aging Bichons

Bichons can live until their late teens with good nutrition, prompt vet care, and a little bit of luck. As your Bichon enters its teen years, take it to the vet at least once a year to discover any health problems early enough to treat them.

Bichons have an average life expectancy of 12-15 years, and with records of Bichons living to be 19-21 years old (in relatively rare instances), Bichon owners are fortunate to have the possibility of a long friendship with their curly-haired best friend. To help our dogs live a long and high-quality life, we must recognize their changing needs in their senior adult years and take special care to do our best to meet them.

But how do we know when our dogs are showing signs of aging?

Some signs of your dog transitioning into his golden years may include:

- Sleeping longer and napping more
- Having more potty accidents
- Visible stiffness in the hips or legs or general weakness
- Playing less, getting tired more quickly during exercise
- Confusion and declining senses
- Cataracts, vision problems, or hearing problems
- Skin tags, moles, and other skin growths anywhere on the body, including the eyes
- Tooth loss or damage
- Irritability or aggression to people or other animals
- Biting (even when a dog has not been a biter in the past)

While this list is not exhaustive, it is an overview of what to look for. But it's important to take *any* changes in your dog's health or behavior seriously and bring them up to your vet quickly. The earlier you detect changes in your Bichon, the earlier you can get help for your special baby.

Common Diseases and Conditions in Bichons

In addition to general signs of aging, there are other common diseases or afflictions that owners of senior dogs should be aware of. But while each breed of dog has ailments that are more common for the breed, you cannot rule out the potential for other illnesses and conditions in the Bichon. Here are some diseases that are particularly common for the Bichon Frise breed.

- Hyperadrenocorticism – Also known as Cushing's Disease, this disease manifests as a tumor in the pituitary gland or adrenal gland. Symptoms of Cushing's Disease include:
  - Increased thirst or hunger
  - Panting
  - Distended belly
  - Thin or discolored skin, with possible hair loss, or possible bruising
  - Having accidents in the house
  - Muscle weakness

The frequent use of certain medications can contribute to the development of Cushing's Disease. Take your pet to the vet if you have reason to believe that your middle-aged or senior dog has developed the condition. Your doctor will do a physical exam and review your dog's medical and prescription history, as well as run any needed tests to determine the diagnosis. The vet may recommend changing current medications, as well as adding a medication to specifically treat the disease. The medication can be costly, and you should expect to visit the vet more frequently to manage the medicine and the disease.

- **Diabetes** – Bichons get diabetes more than most breeds. Heredity and obesity both can contribute to the likelihood of your Bichon getting diabetes. Diabetes is a serious condition that can increase hunger, thirst, and the frequency of urination. To treat diabetes, oral medications and daily injectables are often required. Your vet may also recommend weight loss and dietary changes and restrictions. There is no cure for diabetes.

- **Obesity** – Weight management is essential for healthy living. Since obesity can contribute to the likelihood of heart disease, diabetes, joint problems, and other issues, weight management is an essential aspect of preventing disease and injury. Being overweight is not only a risk factor for disease, but it is tiring for your dog of any age.

Photo Courtesy of Nicole Provenzano

- **Cataracts** – Cataracts often develop slowly, making it hard to notice them easily. Sometimes we don't even notice that our dog's eyesight is beginning to fail. Cataracts cause the lens to become hazy, making it difficult to see and can lead to permanent loss of sight over time. If your dog was once great at catching treats, but now struggles to make a good catch, he might be having vision problems. Since cataracts can be hereditary, they can't always be prevented. However, it is advisable to provide shade for your dog on sunny days to prevent damage from UV light. Cataracts can sometimes be treated with surgery, and with eye drops for maintenance and comfort.

- **Bladder and kidney problems** – Incontinence, leaking or dribbling urine, blood in the urine, and urinary tract infections are all relatively common issues with senior dogs, and typically easy to recognize quickly if your dog is having accidents in the home (especially if the accidents are in strange places). But not all dogs with bladder problems will have accidents in the home that will alert you that something is wrong. As your dog ages, check your dog's urine stream for pus or blood. Bladder infections and bladder stones can be very painful, and without your knowledge, your dog could be suffering in silence.

- **Liver disease** – Bichons are more likely than most other breeds to have a congenital liver disease, called a liver shunt, which decreases blood flow to the liver, thus decreasing the functioning of the liver. But in older Bichons, liver disease can be caused by a variety of factors including prescription drug side effects, consumption of toxins, tumors, infection, or leptospirosis. Symptoms of liver problems may include jaundice, fluid retention, increased thirst and urination, and seizures.

- **Patellar luxation or hip dysplasia (CHD)** – Knees and hips are common problems in many mammals, and even with the small size of the Bichon, they still experience patellar luxation, which is the movement of the knee out of place, as well as hip dysplasia, which is often seen in much larger breeds. If you notice problems while your dog is running, such as lifting up a leg, or pain and muscle weakness in the hips, contact your vet. Medication or surgery may be suggested.

- **Epilepsy** – Epilepsy affects about 1% of the dog population. Signs of epilepsy include falling, shaking, twitching, tongue chewing, and lack of general muscle control. If you think your dog is having a seizure, move him away from anything that could hurt him, maintain a safe distance from his mouth so you don't get bit, and stay calm. While it may be tempting to cradle your dog, this is not advised because he needs to cool down, and he could bite. Instead, turn on a fan and put cool water on your dog's paw pads. Let your vet know if you witness a seizure and record when it occurred and how long it lasted. Depending on the frequency and severity of the seizure the vet may want to put your dog on a daily medication.

- **Spinal cord injuries** – Spinal cord injuries in Bichons are more likely to occur in the neck vertebrae. If your dog is suddenly unable to walk or do his normal activities, or is showing obvious signs of pain, he could have a spinal cord injury. To help prevent these types of injuries, do not allow your dog to jump down from high furniture and provide a ramp, stairs, or a boost up whenever possible.

- **Heart disease** – Heart failure is the leading cause of death in senior Bichons. To help prevent heart disease, keep your Bichon lean and active. Avoid giving him human food no matter how cute he acts when he gets it! Feed him a heart healthy diet and supplement with omega 3 fatty acids. Keep your dog's teeth clean and take him for dental cleanings. If you begin to notice that your dog is out of breath more easily or more easily fatigued, take your Bichon to the doc for a heart checkup.

Illness and Injury Prevention

There is a deep satisfaction in knowing we are doing all we can to keep our dogs safe and healthy. In the long run, preventative care and proactive pet ownership will be worth every dollar or minute you spend on it. Why solve a problem when you can prevent it from occurring?

Early detection – Pay attention to changes in the way your dog walks, runs, and plays. Notice when he shows signs of pain or discomfort while sitting still or in motion. If your Bichon whines, whimpers, cries, or pulls away or refuses to let you touch an area, there is usually a problem.

Running needed tests – Vets are your ally and are highly trained. But even with that training, diagnosing still takes time, effort, and money. We can't expect them to "fix" what is wrong with our dogs until they know what they are treating. Do your best to support your vet's recommendations. If that isn't possible, find out what is essential and be realistic about what your vet can do to help if only limited information is available to make a diagnosis.

Offering proper meds – Medicine management can be cumbersome. Be organized with your pet's meds. Set a daily reminder to administer the medications and use a pill organizer if needed. Always keep the original pill bottles in a safe place in case you need to reference them for any reason.

Choosing quality treats – As dogs age, we tend to want to spoil them more than ever. We sometimes see them as invincible because we remember the time that they ate the family lasagna and didn't get sick, so we think, "why not give them the steak trimmings" and then we are surprised when they are lethargic or vomiting. In order to keep our dogs in tip top shape, we need to refrain from loading them down with fatty, sugary, or generally unhealthy treats.

Staying active and socialized – The concept of "use it or lose it" is not just a cliché. Dogs who are kept inside and on the couch all day will find it harder to get up and move about as they age. Yet there are dogs that seem years younger than their age, and when you speak to their owners, you will typically learn that they have been very active with their dogs throughout their lives, taking them on walks and hikes and keeping a regular exercise routine with them.

Beware of heights – Activity is your dog's friend. But heights can be his nemesis. Senior dogs typically have decreased bone density, causing fragile bones that can lead to fractures in even minor accidents. A fall from a senior dog can be extremely dangerous, so make sure to limit your pup's chances of falling from anything more than 18-24 inches off the ground. Provide safe, non-slip stairs or ramps for climbing. Wood surfaces outdoors can be very slick when wet so add textured tread to decks and steps as needed. If your dog has difficulty maneuvering stairs, use child gates at the top or bottom of stairs to remove this risk. Groom your pet on the floor or on low surfaces (like the couch or a cot) and make sure to hold your dog when he is on the exam table at the vet.

Cuddling, petting, and grooming – This is one of the perks of being a Bichon owner! I love sitting with my boy and petting him. But this snuggle time can also be productive. This is the perfect time to palpate your dog's body for sore muscles or limbs, taking note of his pulling his limb or paw away. Massage alongside the spine and do a little brushing or combing. Does he act normal and seem to enjoy it or is he wiggling away from you? A dog's body language is a series of cues, telling you how he is feeling and what he might need from you.

We cannot prevent all injuries or illnesses, no matter how diligent and aware we are, and no matter how much time and love we put into pet ownership and care. We have to be prepared for the reality that our Bichons, like us, will get sick or hurt, despite our best efforts to protect them.

Basics of Senior Dog Care

Your aging dog needs you now more than ever! You know him best and you are his very best advocate and provider. Staying in tune with your Bichon's needs will be a comfort to both of you and will help add to your dog's confidence as he experiences changes in his body and mind.

Here are some tips for caring for your senior dog:

Consistency in care – Stay on schedule for all vet appointments and stay up to date with vaccines and dental care. Carefully consider all recommended treatments from your vet before declining them. While you might not be able to afford all the care suggested to you, make sure that you understand what your doctor is suggesting for your dog and why. If you can't do expensive tests, ask the vet if there are affordable alternatives for care.

Comfort as he ages – Pay attention to your dog's changing skin, teeth, eyes, appetite, energy level, and signs of pain. Help him ease into old age by doing your best to see what is going on and addressing it. If your dog can no longer get onto the couch or his favorite chair, get him a quality bed he can enjoy and that supports his joints, and put it by your feet. If the food your dog is eating is causing excessive gas or loose stools, consider making a change. Your dog will appreciate you showing concern for his comfort level, even if he can't tell you in words.

Changing needs – As your aging dog experiences joint pain or decreased mobility, consider providing stairs to help him get on the bed, or a ramp to

get in the car. Consider giving him regular gentle massages to help ease achy muscles. Try chilling his water if he isn't showing interest in room temperature water. Try adding blueberries or a scrambled egg to his food occasionally to keep him interested in food. Consider taking vacations closer to home or taking your dog with you, if he is too stressed or upset when you are away. What has worked in the past for your dog may not work as well anymore. By staying in tune with your dog, and keeping an open and creative mindset, you can help your pup get more joy out of his golden years.

Consult as needed – When your concerns are beyond your scope of knowledge, ability, or resources, consult with your vet, an animal behaviorist, or even online social groups for Bichon owners. Sometimes your vet may refer you to a specialist for ophthalmology, oncology, or other veterinary specialties. There may be medical concerns that your regular vet does not handle. Keep an open mind about letting the specialists increase the quality of life for your dog.

Grooming

When taking your senior Bichon to the groomer, I recommend only choosing an experienced and well-trained groomer. Ask them about their training in working with senior dogs and request recommendations from their clients. Check out their online reviews for any red flags.

Here are some additional tips for making grooming a positive experience for your senior dog:

- Choose a groomer you know and trust or one that has been highly recommended to you, or one with a strong reputation for successfully working with senior or special needs dogs.

- Meet the groomer and ask to see their setup for grooming your dog. Make sure that there isn't a risk for your dog to fall and get injured.

- Keep your dog well-groomed at home so that the day at the groomer is less stressful.

- Ask the groomer how they handle issues like:

  - Dementia, confusion, hearing, and vision problems – Confused or impaired dogs often become nervous more easily because they are not fully cognizant of what is happening around them. They may become startled more easily if they don't know what to expect. This could make them tremble, cry, squirm, or even bite. The groomer will need experience caring for geriatric dogs and will need to employ strategies to soothe and calm frightened or confused dogs.

- Mobility issues or difficulty standing – If it is difficult for your dog to stand for long, ask that your pet be groomed sitting or lying down for as long as possible and ask if it is possible for someone to assist in holding him if needed.

- Increased need for potty breaks – Your senior pup will likely need a couple of chances to potty. When you arrive for your appointment, make sure to remind the receptionist or groomer of this need.

- Water breaks – Most people assume that their dog will get water while they are at the groomer but this is not always the case. And when dogs are stressed, they become thirsty more quickly. Make sure to ask that your dog get water while he is being groomed. I always request this each time that I take my dogs for grooming. And I always tip the groomer and receptionist so that they are more inclined to give my dogs care that may not be standard for all dogs.

- Comfort breaks – Your dog may benefit from short breaks.

- Ask your groomer to check your dog for any skin issues when grooming. An experienced groomer should bring any concerns to your attention.

- Ask your groomer and vet about calming treats to help make the visit a little easier.

- Consider hiring a mobile groomer to come to your house and discuss the benefits of you being present for the grooming. This could help calm your pet, but he may also do better without you standing right by him.

- Wait while your Bichon is being groomed if you are able. If staying at the groomer all day is hard on your dog, get a set appointment time and stay with him while he is groomed. Then you can get him home sooner so he can relax and enjoy his fresh new hairdo in his favorite comfy spot.

Keeping your Bichon in the habit of being groomed and being gently handled will help reduce anxiety and stress. While it may be tempting to shield your dog from all possible stressors, remember that isolation can actually increase the likelihood of becoming stressed. Keep your dog well socialized and exposed to a variety of situations as long as it is safe and recommended by your vet.

If taking your Bichon to the groomer is truly too much stress, consider learning how to groom him at home. It may take a few hours, or even a few sessions over a few days to get it all done, but this can be a bonding time for you and your pet and there is great satisfaction in offering your dog the comfort he needs at this stage in his life.

Nutrition

Because your dog's senior years may come with their own unique challenges, it's important to continue to feed your Bichon a high-quality dog food. Senior Bichons will have a slower metabolism meaning that they will require fewer calories, as well as increased protein, fiber, and probiotics. As soon as your dog begins to slow down, or around age 8 if no obvious signs of aging have begun to show yet, discuss your vet's suggestions for making changes (if any) to your Bichon's diet.

Here are some helpful tips for feeding your senior Bichon:

- **Limit treats** and consider only giving your dog supplements as "treats" and only offering nonessential treats occasionally. Older dogs can get picky if we are not careful not to spoil them. Treats should compose a very small part of your dog's diet, so be sure not to get into the habit of over-treating, even if your dog shows little or no interest in his usual food. If this occurs, contact your vet instead of compensating a balanced meal with treats that cannot meet your dog's complex nutritional needs.

- **Limit fats** to what is recommended for your dog's age. I haven't met a dog that doesn't love fat from a steak or bacon grease on their food, but high fat foods are risky for your senior Bichon because it can cause vomiting, diarrhea, and even pancreatitis. While we enjoy watching our pups enjoy an immensely tasty meal (often laden with fat), we will not enjoy watching them feel sick after eating these foods that are difficult to digest and too high in calories for their slowing metabolism. If your dog consumes a great deal of fat in one sitting (on purpose or because your dog is a sneaky trash digger like mine) watch for signs of illness, indigestion, fever, hunched back and general malaise and contact your vet immediately. Pancreatitis, left untreated, can be fatal for your dog. Do not attempt to substitute veterinary care with home care for your Bichon if pancreatitis is suspected.

- **Limit risks** to your senior Bichon's health by paying attention to potentially hidden ingredients. Do not just look at the front of the bag, box or can, which is not required to list all the ingredients, or can be misleading. If your dog is allergic to any specific ingredient, check the nutritional information and never make assumptions about ingredients that could adversely impact your dog's health. A beef meal can contain chicken. A sweet potato treat may contain corn. Labels are often misleading. Read carefully.

- **Add a probiotic** to your senior dog's diet to aid in digestion and comfort for your dog. Probiotics can come in capsules, soft treats, powders or even yogurts. Talk to your vet about what is right for your dog, and as always, read the ingredients before feeding your dog anything new.

- **Avoid constipation** by focusing on hydration and healthy fiber. A senior dog may need more water to stay hydrated and to keep his digestive system working properly. If your dog doesn't seem to want his water, trying chilling the water or adding ice cubes to it, or add water to his food. You can increase his fiber intake by adding wheat germ or flaxseed to his food, or by offering cut up green beans, broccoli, carrots, or apples. You can serve the produce raw or steamed, depending on what your pet prefers. Canned plain pumpkin can also aid in digestion. Add a bit to your dog's food for flavor.

- **Watch for chewing issues**. Digestion begins in the mouth when your dog properly chews his food. If his teeth are missing or damaged, or if he has other oral or jaw issues, chewing may become hard or painful, and this may cause his eating to slow drastically. Consider downsizing to a smaller kibble, cutting the produce into smaller bites or steaming it, or adding a small amount of warm water or diluted broth to the food. Making the food more manageable can make eating more enjoyable for your little Bichon and make digestion easier on your dog.

- **Talk to the vet about weight management.** Sometimes, despite our best efforts, our dogs continue to gain weight. If this occurs, there could be an underlying cause and the vet may want to do some bloodwork, check their thyroid levels, or run other tests. Sometimes, diet alone is not enough to maintain optimal weight. Never drop below the recommended daily caloric intake for your dog unless guided to do so by the vet. It's better to discuss all options with the vet than to risk underfeeding your dog in order to help him reach a goal weight.

If you decide to make changes to your dog's diet, make one change at a time. A total revamp overnight is likely to do more harm than good, as sudden dietary changes can be irritating to your dog's digestive system. Go slowly, and watch for any undesirable effects before making other changes. This way, if something does upset your dog's stomach, you will know right away what did it. Give your dog a couple of weeks to adjust to a change before considering making any more changes.

If your dog is experiencing other potential digestive issues (with or without changes to his diet) such as bloody stools, loose or watery stools, mucus in his stool, constipation, vomiting (on an empty or full stomach), bloating, excessive gas, weight loss, or even fever or lethargy, please contact your vet. An isolated incident of many of these issues may not amount to a serious illness in your dog, but a combination of any of them, or a repeated instance of any one of them may indicate mild to serious digestive issues (or other health issues), and you should contact your vet, or go to the emergency vet immediately.

Exercise

When you think of exercise for your aging dog, think beyond your typical walk around the block (but that is good too!). Variety in his activities and varying the stimulus will help keep your dog interested, mentally engaged, and actively participating in life.

Here are some ways to make life fun and exciting for your aging pooch:

- **Mental stimulation** – "An object in motion stays in motion. An object at rest stays at rest." Newton's Law of Motion serves as an analogy for our dogs' mental and physical health. To keep our dogs mentally and physically "in motion" we must continue to challenge them with new games, different concepts, fresh faces, and unexpected places.

  - Buy puzzles and games to get your dog's mental acuity in action

  - Play games like hide and seek (hide your dog's favorite bone and have him try to root it out), let him sniff new places and strange things, introduce him to toys he has never tried before.

  - Teach him something new. Dogs love to be challenged and enjoy pleasing their humans. If your Bichon can "shake," maybe it's time that he learns how to "high 5." If you're a bit of a party animal yourself, try teaching your little partner to dance. Even if he doesn't quite master the trick, I bet both of you will enjoy practicing.

- **Short walks** – If your dog can predict your walking or jogging route, consider taking a different one. Take your dog on new trails at new parks. Take him on a city walk if he is a country pup and try a meandering walk in the country if your city dwelling Bichon has seen enough fire hydrants for a bit.

- **Car rides** – Take your dog with you when you don't have to get out of the car. Take your dog on a drive along the coastline with fresh air streaming in the sunroof. Take him to a dog deli or bakery, or to a friend's house for a cookout.

- **Hydrotherapy** – Take your senior dog for a dip in the pool (life jacket is a must if you don't know your dog's swimming skills or if he doesn't have complete mobility). Take him to a hydrotherapy center for a relaxing whirlpool session to increase circulation or a walk on the underwater treadmill to increase his mobility. Warm water can decrease joint and muscle pain as well.

- **Warm up and cool down** – Give your senior dog more time to warm up for strenuous activities. Walk a bit longer before jogging. Play a bit before swimming. And after an intense (for him) workout, allow your senior dog ample time to decrease his heart rate and cool down their muscles before hopping into the car, or sprawling out in front of the television.

- **Passive stretching** – Passive stretching is stretching you do to your dog by gently moving his body in a way to elongate the muscles in a therapeutic and useful way. This can be part of the warm-up or cool-down, or it can be done independently of exercise. Stretching is essential for aging people and dogs alike. Lay your dog on his side and very gently stretch the front and back leg that he is not lying on. To be sure that you do not overextend the muscles, keep your dog's limbs parallel to the floor. Then reverse your dog and repeat on the other side. Try gently "bicycling" your dog's front and back legs while he lies cradled on his back in your lap.

Playing unique games, learning new tricks, and staying in the habit of exercise should be enjoyable bonding experiences for you and your Bichon, serving to strengthen the trust that you have developed during your time together. These activities will serve your intelligent, curious, active senior dog well into the "winter season" of his life.

Common Old-Age Ailments

No one, not even your vet, can fully predict the health and wellness of your Bichon as he ages. However, there are common old-age ailments that you might see in the future. Here are some changes and ailments your senior Bichon may experience.

- **General fitness** – Older dogs are more susceptible to injury and joint pain. You may notice that your dog's general appearance changes such that he looks thinner or less muscular.

- **Immune system** – Senior dogs may have weakened immune systems, placing them at a higher risk for communicable diseases. Keep your dog up to date on vaccines and be careful about putting him in situations that could elevate his risk of illness. Older dogs may take longer to recover from illnesses.

- **Nutrition and Metabolism** – As your dog's metabolism slows down, he will begin to need fewer calories. For this reason, many senior dogs can become overweight if we don't monitor their caloric intake and food quality closely. Your vet may recommend switching your Bichon to a lower calorie dog food. Keeping your Bichon at his ideal weight will help him continue to stay active for as long as possible. Overweight dogs tend to nap more, sleep longer, and move more slowly.

- **Fatigue** – Senior dogs enjoy their cat naps more and more. Taking them on walks and keeping them moderately active will help keep them from tiring too easily. Exercise combats obesity that will often lead to other health issues and discomfort.

- **Temperature control** – Be mindful when taking your senior dog out in the heat or cold. He may have a harder time regulating his body temperatures due to changes in his skin quality and elasticity. Choose appropriate times of day to take your pup outside and dress him appropriately for the weather. Senior dogs often appreciate a jacket or sweater to help keep them warm in colder weather. Consider getting boots for your pup to wear in the cold or snow as his paws may crack and split more easily. Not only is this painful, but it can increase the chance of infection. Provide shade and water on hot or humid days. Shorten your dog's outdoor time and check for signs of breathing issues, heat stroke, or a sudden drop in body temperature.

- **Skin and coat** – Older dogs may experience hair thinning or loss, dryer and duller coats, irritated skin or rashes, or general dryness. Your senior dog may need supplements to help combat skin and coat issues and you may need to try more gentle products for bathing him, including a nourishing conditioner. Due to your older dog's more fragile skin, do not bathe him too frequently (once a month is a good guide for older Bichons, but you can adjust to your dog's needs). If you notice flakiness or itchiness, stop using the products you are using and contact your vet for advice.

- **Dental health** – Tooth decay, tooth loss, and gum disease or common ailments for senior pups, which can lead to more serious health issues if not treated. Brush your dog's teeth regularly and pay attention to his dental wellbeing so you will be aware when changes occur. Discuss dental cleaning with your vet to determine how often you should schedule appointments. If you notice your dog not eating, check his teeth and gums. Sometimes dogs stop eating when they have swollen gums, a broken tooth, and ulcers in their mouth.

- **Bladder issues** – Your senior dog may experience bladder incontinence, bladder infections, bladder and kidney stones, and other urinary tract issues. You may notice your dog having pee accidents in your house, notice blood in his urine, or note that he is having difficulty emptying his bladder. If you notice any issues that could be bladder related, see your vet immediately. Your dog may require medication or other treatments, and may need a change in diet to help prevent future bladder problems. Bladder infections can lead to subtle or major behavioral changes in your dog. These changes should prompt concern and action.

Photo Courtesy of
Marnie Williams

When It's Time to Say Goodbye

There is no failsafe formula for knowing when it is time to say goodbye to our beloved pets. Most of us hope that our dogs will pass peacefully in their sleep without pain or fear, and that ideal is often the basis for our decisions moving forward. We all, in the end, want to offer our calming reassurance and love, as well as physical comfort, to the dog who has been by our side for so long.

In my time working in an animal clinic, I have met many clients who have made an appointment to discuss their pet's end of life. During these visits, the clients ask the vet questions like:

- "How do we know how our dog is feeling?"
- "Is he in pain?"
- "Is he suffering?"
- "Is he scared?"
- "Does he understand what's happening?"
- "How do I know when to let go?"

As much as your vet would like to answer all of your questions, they can't always tell you exactly how your dog is feeling physically, mentally, or emotionally. Instead, your vet will likely rely on the information that you are able to provide about your dog's quality of life, to then help make recommendations to you on how much quality time your dog has left with you.

Quality of life is defined as the total comfort or happiness experienced by someone. All in all, quality of life assesses how happy and healthy your dog truly is, and what continued enjoyment he could receive moving forward. Here are some questions (using the acronym COMFORT) that may help you and your vet reach a conclusion that will offer you comfort and confidence:

- **Chronic problems** – How severe are your dog's health issues? Vision, hearing, arthritis, obesity, weight loss, dementia, cancer, chronic pain, and more are all issues that may be part of, or the root cause of, chronic problems affecting your dog's wellness.
- **Owner's observations** – Does your dog seem like himself? Can he do the things he's always enjoyed, or does he isolate himself from you and the family most of the time? Do you constantly worry about your pet's health and wellness, or are you able to relax while away from the home without extreme worry?

- **Mobility** – Can your Bichon walk easily, or does he fall often? Is getting up and down painful? Does he shake when he walks? Is moving a burden for him?

- **Food and water** – Does your dog eat fairly well or do you have to hand-feed him or prepare special meals just to get him to eat a little? Does he drink water or is he frequently dehydrated? Is your dog having diarrhea or vomiting after eating? Is he losing weight from his disinterest or inability to eat?

- **Overall happiness** – Is your dog enjoying time with the family, wagging his tail and interacting? Or does he seem mostly tired or uncomfortable? Is his pain managed well at least 75% of the time? Does he seem anxious, upset, and confused to the point where you are scared to leave him alone even for short periods of time? Do you often feel sorry for your dog?

- **Respiration** – Is breathing a chore and laborious for your dog? Does your dog suffer frequent bouts of coughing or wheezing? Is it difficult for him to catch his breath?

- **Tidiness** – Is your dog having frequent accidents inside? Is he able to potty on his own and let you know when he has to go? Or is he lying on soiled bedding with little or no concern for cleanliness? Does he groom himself at all, or does he require frequent or constant cleaning from you?

There is no perfect time to say goodbye, but with careful consideration we can think through the quality of life for our pets. If you have reached the conclusion that it is time to say goodbye to your dear friend, take time to say goodbye alone, and give others in your family the time to do so when possible.

If you are taking your dog to the vet to be put to sleep, take a blanket or a bed to make him feel comfortable. Decide in advance if you would like to stay with your dog while he is in the process of passing. You can request that your dog be sedated before he is medicated with a lethal dose of sodium pentobarbital. Sedation can help to keep a dog from moving during the insertion of the sodium pentobarbital and help reduce the chances of it blowing out a vein. The medication will slow down the heart rate until it stops gently. Your dog may experience involuntary movements or urination/defecation. This is normal. Your dog will not feel any pain during the process.

You may be able to choose to put your dog to sleep at home, for his comfort and your own. But if you think that this will only upset you or your family more, please take your dog to the vet for the procedure.

If you are legally able, you can choose to bury your dog at home. You can also take your dog to be buried in a pet cemetery. Most people, however, choose cremation for their dogs. You can choose a communal or a private cremation. With a communal cremation, your dog will be cremated with other animals. If you want to get your dog's ashes returned to you, you will need to choose a private cremation. If your pet dies at home, but you would like him cremated privately, then wrap him carefully and put his name (first and last) on the wrapping. Contact your vet to let them know you are on your way. Some communities offer pick-up services for deceased animals, but not all. Call your vet or your local animal shelter for more information on services available in your area.

Many animal clinics will take the time to get an ink or plaster imprint of your dog's paw. If this is highly important to you, it's important you confirm in advance that this is a service that is offered.

Grieving

It is common for your other animals to struggle with the loss of their friend. Be patient with them and do not rush the process. They may become more reclusive or more demanding. They may sleep more and eat less. They may avoid fun activities and avoid your deceased dog's favorite spot. They may become sad, irritable, or even aggressive. Be attentive and thoughtful in your care towards your other pets, not rushing to force them into more than they are ready for. If your pets become physically ill from their grief, contact your vet.

Helping your children grieve can be particularly painful to endure. There are age-appropriate books and coloring books for younger children. Older children and teens will grieve in their own way too. Some will grieve only in private. Having a special photo of your pet framed and telling sweet stories about your lost loved one can help everyone begin the process of healing.

Take time for yourself to reflect and grieve. Losing a beloved pet is physically and emotionally painful. I have seen many Bichon owners grieving the recent passing of their longtime friend, and my heart always goes out to them. All we can do is enjoy each day with our Bichons and give them lots of love. This is always time well spent. And when it is time for them to come to rest, may we give them the peace and love they deserve. And remember, the only cure for grief is to grieve. It is a process. Take your time.

Made in the USA
Las Vegas, NV
11 September 2021